FLOWERS

— IN —

CROSS STITCH

Jana Hauschild Lindberg

CASSELL

A CASSELL BOOK

First published 1992
by Cassell
Villiers House
41/47 Strand
London
WC2N 5JE

First published in paperback 1993

Distributed in the United States
by Sterling Publishing Co., Inc.
387 Park Avenue South, New York, New York 10016-8810

Distributed in Australia
by Capricorn Link (Australia) Pty Ltd
P.O. Box 665, Lane Cove, NSW 2066

British Library Cataloguing-in-Publication Data
A catalogue record for this book is available from the British Library

ISBN 0-304-34129-0
    0-304-34359-5 (paperback)

Typeset by MS Filmsetting Limited, Frome, Somerset

Printed and bound in Portugal by Printer Portuguesa

Contents

Introduction

*P*eople all around the world love flowers. This is the reason why I have concentrated on flowers in this book. All kinds of flowers are included: garden, wild, exotic, and even field flowers which can be found in the humblest places, single ones or bunches, naturalistic or stylized. There are pretty floral designs to decorate your home or just small ideas to liven up an old blouse, collar or scarf. You can make a personal sampler by choosing your favourites from the numerous designs in the book. Why not a sampler for a new-born member of the family? There are countless ways to make use of the charted flower designs.

Counted Cross Stitch Technique and Projects

Counted cross stitch is one of the simplest forms of embroidery. It consists of a series of crossed stitches embroidered on an evenweave fabric over the intersection of the horizontal and vertical threads. The stitches are worked following a chart. Each cross stitch is indicated by a symbol; the different symbols represent different colours (fig. 1). You can work the design as directed in the colour key, or make up your own original colour scheme.

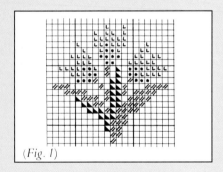

(Fig. 1)

TULIPS

- ⊙ 601 dark pink
- L 603 light pink
- ◣ 987 dark green
- ⊘ 989 light green

The size of a cross stitch design is determined by the type of fabric upon which it is embroidered. Although finished sizes are given for the designs in this book, it is easy to calculate what a different finished size will be by using the following formula:

$$\frac{\text{Finished}}{\text{size}} = \frac{\text{Number of stitches}}{\text{Thread-count of fabric}}$$

For example, let's say you have selected a design that is 42 stitches wide and 98 stitches long and you would like to work on a cloth that has $5\frac{1}{2}$ threads per cm (14 threads per in). The finished width of your design can be determined by dividing the number of stitches (42) by the number of threads ($5\frac{1}{2}$/14), which gives you a design that is 7.5 cm (3 in) wide. For the length, divide the number of stitches (98) by the thread count ($5\frac{1}{2}$/14) to find out that the design will be 17.5 cm (7 in) long. If you feel this size is too large, try switching to a linen cloth which has 10 threads per cm (25 threads per in). The size in that case would be approximately 4 cm ($1\frac{1}{2}$ in) wide by 10 cm (4 in) long. Use this formula to decide quickly which thread count of fabric is best for you to use.

MATERIALS

FABRIC

You can use any evenweave fabric made from cotton, linen, wool or synthetic blends. Cotton and linen fabrics are the most widely used. Counted thread fabrics specially woven for cross stitch, such as Aida or Hardanger, are available in many needlecraft shops, although these are limited in colour range. Aida fabric is cotton and can be bought in three sizes: $4\frac{1}{2}$, $5\frac{1}{2}$ or 7 threads per cm (11, 14 or 18 threads per in). Hardanger cloth is available in linen or cotton. If you would like to embroider on an unusually coloured fabric, try using linen which is available in most fabric shops. When using linen, one has to take into account the inevitable slubs and inconsistencies that occur in the weave; this is why it is best to work counted cross stitch over two or more threads on linen fabric (see fig. 7). Thirty-count linen will give much the same effect as working on 14-count Aida cloth.

The materials used for the designs given in this book include linen and Aida. Linen measures are in threads. Aida measures are in stitches. Please note the following:

10 threads per cm = 25 per in

8 threads per cm = 20 per in

6 threads per cm = 15 per in

$5\frac{1}{2}$ stitches per cm = $13\frac{1}{2}$ per in

$4\frac{1}{2}$ stitches per cm = 11 per in

THREADS AND YARNS

Six-strand cotton embroidery floss is ideal for counted cross stitch because the floss can be separated into the exact number of strands that provide the correct amount of coverage. Use thread or yarn that is the same thickness as the threads of the fabric you are embroidering. For flatter designs, separate the strands of floss and work with two strands in your needle. If you wish to create a more textured effect, use more strands. You can also use silk or metallic threads, Danish Flower Thread, pearl cotton, even crewel wool, depending on the

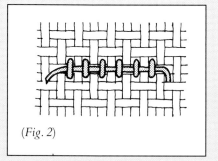

(*Fig. 2*)

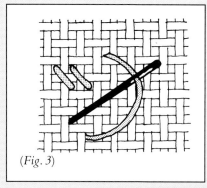

(*Fig. 3*)

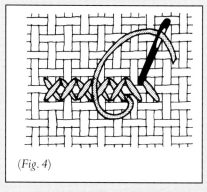

(*Fig. 4*)

thread count of your fabric. To add some sparkle to a design, mix one strand of metallic thread with two strands of embroidery floss. Throughout this book I have referred to DMC six-strand embroidery floss. A conversion chart at the end of this chapter shows at a glance where you can make substitutions with flosses manufactured by two other companies: Royal Mouliné, or Coats/Bates Anchor.

EQUIPMENT

NEEDLES
Use a small blunt tapestry needle, size number 24 or 26, to avoid splitting the fabric threads.

HOOP
Work with a small round embroidery hoop which consists of an inner ring and an adjustable outer ring that tightens by turning a screw.

SCISSORS
You must have a pair of small sharp embroidery scissors for cutting threads and a pair of sharp fabric shears for cutting out the fabric.

TECHNIQUE

Depending upon the gift project that you would like to make (see instructions at the end of this chapter), cut your fabric to the desired size plus about 2.5 cm (1 in) around each of the edges. Overcast the edges of the fabric to prevent unravelling by hemming, zigzagging on the sewing machine or whipstitching. Find the centre of the fabric by folding it in half crosswise and lengthwise; mark the centre point with a small stitch. Then find the centre of your design (usually indicated on the charts by arrows). Do not begin your design at the centre; instead, count the number of squares on the chart from the centre point to the top, then count the same number of squares to the top of your fabric and work your first stitch there. Work the design in horizontal rows of colour from left to right. Place the fabric in the embroidery hoop so that it is taut. Adjust the tension as you work so that the fabric is always firmly held.

Begin stitching by leaving a length of waste thread on the back of the work, securing it with your first few stitches. Fig. 2 shows how the waste thread is secured on the wrong side of the work. Insert your needle into the holes of the fabric, working one slanted stitch over the intersection of two threads from lower right to upper left as shown in fig. 3. Continue working the required number of slanting stitches across the row, following the symbols on the chart. Then work back across the row, making slanting stitches from lower left to upper right to finish each cross stitch as shown in fig. 4. (In Denmark and America, stitches are worked from lower left to upper right, then crossed from lower right to upper left. It makes no difference which way you stitch, as long as all the stitches are crossed in the same direction.)

When you are working a vertical row of stitches, cross each stitch in turn as shown in fig. 5. To end a line of stitching, finish your last stitch and keep the needle and thread on the wrong side of the work. Wiggle the

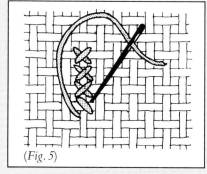

(*Fig. 5*)

point of the needle beneath a few threads on the wrong side and pull the thread through as shown in fig. 6; clip off the excess thread so that the ends will not show through on the right side of the work.

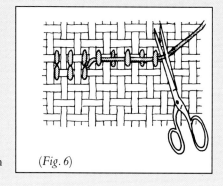

(*Fig. 6*)

If you are working on linen, or if you wish to make larger stitches, work over two sets of threads in each direction as shown in fig. 7. Your first few stitches may be difficult, but once you have established a row of stitches, you'll have no trouble counting two threads instead of one.

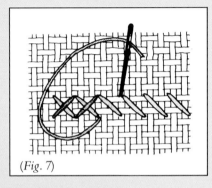

(Fig. 7)

BACKSTITCH

Backstitch is very commonly used in conjunction with counted cross stitch to outline, delineate features or emphasize a portion of the design. Work the backstitches from one hole to the next in a horizontal, vertical or diagonal direction; see fig. 8.

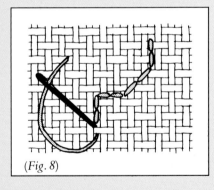

(Fig. 8)

WORKING WITH WASTE CANVAS

Counted cross stitch can be worked on non-evenweave fabrics by using a non-interlock waste canvas. Select a canvas with a stitch count of the desired size. Cut the canvas slightly larger than the finished size of your design. Baste the canvas to your chosen fabric in the area you wish to embroider. Using a crewel or chenille needle, work the design over the canvas. As you work, pass the needle straight up and down through the

fabric and canvas; take great care not to catch the canvas threads in your embroidery. When the embroidery is finished, remove the basting and dampen the canvas thoroughly using a warm wet towel. Gently pull out the canvas threads one by one. Press the finished embroidery.

SMALL QUICK PROJECTS

BOOKMARK

Cut piece of evenweave fabric about 15 × 5 cm (6 × 2 in). Overcast the raw edges. Embroider a small motif or border design on the fabric; gently press the finished embroidery. Trim away the overcast edge. Carefully draw away threads from the cut edges, creating a 6 mm ($\frac{1}{4}$ in) fringe.

GIFT TAG, PLACECARD or NAME LABEL

Cut evenweave fabric 2.5 cm (1 in) larger than desired finished size. Overcast the raw edges. Embroider a small motif on the fabric; gently press the finished embroidery. Cut away excess fabric, leaving about 13 mm ($\frac{1}{2}$ in) all around the edge of the design. Carefully draw away threads from the cut edges, creating a 6 mm ($\frac{1}{4}$ in) fringe. Glue the wrong side of the design to a rectangular piece of card.

PINCUSHION OR SACHET

Cut evenweave fabric about 2.5 cm (1 in) larger than desired finished size (or more, depending upon the size of the design). Overcast the raw edges. Embroider a small motif on the fabric, gently press the finished embroidery. Cut away excess fabric

to desired size. Cut a matching piece of fabric for the back; stitch together with right sides facing and raw edges even, making a 6 mm ($\frac{1}{4}$ in) seam and leaving an opening for turning. Turn to the right side and stuff with kapok, fibrefill or potpourri until plump. Fold in raw edges at the opening and slipstitch opening closed.

MATCHBOX COVER

Embroider a small motif on a piece of evenweave fabric; gently press the finished embroidery. Cut away excess fabric to the exact size of the matchbox you wish to decorate. Glue the wrong side of the design to the top of the matchbox, making sure the raw edges are securely glued so they do not unravel.

POCKET

Using a commercial pocket pattern, cut one pocket from evenweave fabric, adding the appropriate seam allowances. Embroider a small motif in the centre of the fabric; gently press the finished embroidery. Cut a matching piece of fabric for the lining; stitch together with right sides facing, leaving an opening for turning. Turn to the right side, fold in raw edges at the opening, and slipstitch the opening closed. Press carefully. Topstitch the edges of the pocket if desired, then sew to the front of a blouse or skirt with small slipstitches.

TIE OR COLLAR

Read the earlier instructions for working with waste canvas. Select a small design. Centre the waste canvas on a tie or collar and baste into place. Work the design over the canvas, then remove the canvas threads as directed. Press the finished embroidery gently.

HANDKERCHIEF

Read the earlier instructions for working with waste canvas. Select a small design. Position the waste canvas in the corner of a handkerchief and baste in place. Work the design over the canvas, then remove the canvas threads as directed. Press the finished embroidery gently.

T-SHIRT

Read the earlier instructions for working with waste canvas. Select a medium to large design. Centre the waste canvas on the front of a T-shirt and baste in place. Work the design over the canvas, then remove the canvas threads as directed. Press the finished embroidery gently.

BABY'S BIB

Use a piece of evenweave fabric, adding 6 mm ($\frac{1}{4}$ in) all round. Overcast the raw edges. Find the centre of the bib at the neckline; begin working a small design about 2.5 cm (1 in) below the raw neck edge or in the exact centre of the bib front. Gently press the finished embroidery. Trim away overcast edge. Finish the raw edges of the bib with bias binding, leaving excess binding at the back for tying.

CHRISTMAS ORNAMENTS

Cut evenweave fabric about 2.5 cm (1 in) larger than desired finished size. Overcast the raw edges. Embroider a small motif on the fabric; gently press the finished embroidery. Cut away excess fabric to desired size; for a special effect, cut around the shape of the design, leaving a 6 mm ($\frac{1}{4}$ in) seam allowance all around. Cut a matching piece of fabric for the back; stitch together with right sides facing and raw edges even, making a 6 mm

($\frac{1}{4}$ in) seam and leaving an opening for turning. Clip any curved edges. Turn to the right side and stuff with kapok or polyester fibrefill until plump. Fold in raw edges at opening and slipstitch opening closed.

DECORATING THE HOME

WALLHANGING

Calculate the finished size of your design using the formula on page 6; cut evenweave fabric 5 cm (2 in) larger all round than the calculated size. Overcast the raw edges. Find the exact centre of the fabric and the design and count up to the top of the design and fabric. Begin embroidering downward until the design is finished. Carefully press the finished embroidery. Measure 3.8 cm ($1\frac{1}{2}$ in) from the outer edge of the embroidery at the sides and bottom and trim away the excess fabric. Trim away only the overcast edge at the top. Fold the fabric at the side and bottom edges 6 mm ($\frac{1}{4}$ in) to the wrong side, then fold the fabric again 13 mm ($\frac{1}{2}$ in) to the wrong side. Baste, then sew the hem in place with small slipstitches. For the casing at the top edge, press the raw edge 6 mm ($\frac{1}{4}$ in) to the wrong side, then fold down 19 mm ($\frac{3}{4}$ in); stitch in place with small slipstitches. Press gently. Insert a brass or wooden rod through the casing.

TABLE RUNNER

Cut a piece of evenweave fabric 2.5 cm (1 in) larger all around than the desired finished size of your table runner. Overcast the raw edges.

Decide where you wish to place the design. Embroider your chosen design, adding a border all around the table runner if desired. Carefully press the finished embroidery. Cut away excess fabric, leaving 19 mm ($\frac{3}{4}$ in) for hemming. Fold the fabric 6 mm ($\frac{1}{4}$ in) to the wrong side, then fold the fabric again, this time 13 mm ($\frac{1}{2}$ in) to the wrong side. Baste, then sew the hem in place with small slipstitches. Press gently.

CURTAIN TIEBACK OR LAMPSHADE TRIM

Cut evenweave fabric slightly longer than required and wide enough for the design plus 13 mm ($\frac{1}{2}$ in). Overcast the raw edges. Embroider a border design along the centre of the fabric. Gently press the finished embroidery. Cut a matching piece of interfacing and lining. Baste the interfacing to the wrong side of the embroidery. With right sides facing, stitch the lining to the embroidery making a 13 mm ($\frac{1}{2}$ in) seam. Turn right side out and press lightly. For the tieback, fold the raw edges inside and slipstitch in place. Apply Velcro touch-and-close fastener to secure the ends together. For the lampshade trim, fold raw edges at one end to the wrong side. Slipstitch or glue the embroidery around the bottom edge of the lampshade, slipping the raw edges inside the folded edge. Slipstitch to secure.

CURTAIN

Measure your window and make a curtain using an evenweave fabric; the curtain should not be very full. Hem the bottom edge of the curtain, but not the sides. Overcast the raw edges. Begin working a border design in the exact centre of the fabric, just above the hem. Work

FOR THE KITCHEN AND DINING ROOM

outward to each side edge. When finished, hem the side edges of the curtain. Gently press the finished embroidery.

CUSHION

Calculate the finished size of your design using the formula on page 6; cut evenweave fabric 2.5 cm (1 in) larger than the calculated size all around. Overcast the raw edges. Work the design in the centre of the fabric. Carefully press the finished embroidery. Trim away the excess fabric leaving a 13 mm ($\frac{1}{2}$ in) seam allowance all around. Cut a matching piece of fabric for the back. With right sides facing, stitch the back to the front making a 6 mm ($\frac{1}{4}$ in) seam and leaving an opening for turning. Turn to the right side and stuff with kapok or polyester fibrefill until plump. Fold in the raw edges at the opening and slipstitch the opening closed.

BATH TOWEL EDGING

Cut evenweave fabric slightly longer than your towel and wide enough for the design plus 13 mm ($\frac{1}{2}$ in). Overcast the raw edges. Embroider a border design along the centre of the fabric. Gently press the finished embroidery. Trim off the overcast edges. Fold the raw edges of the embroidery 6 mm ($\frac{1}{4}$ in) to the wrong side and baste to your towel; slipstitch securely along each edge.

POTHOLDER

Cut a piece of evenweave fabric about 18–23 cm (7–9 in) square. Overcast the raw edges. Select a design that will fit nicely on the fabric and embroider the design in the centre. Gently press the finished embroidery. Trim off the overcast edges, then cut padding and a back to the same size; use two to three layers of cotton or wool padding (do not use polyester). Sandwich the padding between the embroidery and the back; baste the edges together. Use bias binding to finish the edges of the potholder, allowing excess binding at one corner to make a hanging loop.

SHELF BORDER

Cut evenweave fabric slightly longer than your shelf and wide enough for the design plus 13 mm ($\frac{1}{2}$ in). Overcast the raw edges. Embroider a border design along the centre of the fabric. Gently press the finished embroidery. Trim off the overcast edges. Cut a matching piece of interfacing. Baste the interfacing to the wrong side of the embroidery.

Fold the raw edges of the embroidery 6 mm ($\frac{1}{4}$ in) to the wrong side and secure to the interfacing with small slipstitches. Press lightly. Pin or glue the border to the front of your cupboard shelf.

PLACEMAT

Cut a piece of evenweave fabric 2.5 cm (1 in) larger all round than the desired finished size of your placemat; a good finished size is about 35 × 45 cm ($13\frac{3}{4} \times 17\frac{3}{4}$ in). Overcast the raw edges. Decide where you wish to place the design—an attractive arrangement is to centre the design between the top and bottom edges along the left-hand edge of the fabric. Embroider your chosen design, adding a border all around the placemat if desired. Carefully press the finished embroidery. Cut away excess fabric, leaving 19 mm ($\frac{3}{4}$ in) for hemming. Fold the fabric 6 mm ($\frac{1}{4}$ in) to the wrong side, then fold the fabric again, this time 13 mm ($\frac{1}{2}$ in) to the wrong side. Baste, then sew the hem in place with small slipstitches. Press gently.

ROUND TABLECLOTH OR CENTREPIECE

Calculate the finished size of your design using the formula on page 6; cut evenweave fabric 3.8 cm (1½ in) larger than the calculated size all round. Overcast the raw edges. Find the exact centre of the fabric and the design; mark on fabric with a basting thread. Count from the centre of the graph and the fabric to start the design. Work the graph, which is one-quarter of the design, as shown. Then turn the fabric clockwise and work the next quarter. Continue turning and repeating the quarter pattern twice more until the design is finished. Carefully press the embroidery. Measure 3 cm (1¼ in) away from the outer edge of the embroidery and trim off the excess fabric. Fold the fabric 6 mm (¼ in) to the wrong side twice. Baste, then sew the hem in place with small slipstitches. Press gently.

ROUND DOILY OR TRAY CLOTH

Work as for the tablecloth, but cut your evenweave fabric 2.5 cm (1 in) larger than the calculated size of the project all round.

SIX-STRAND EMBROIDERY COTTON (FLOSS) CONVERSION CHART

Key: T = Possible substitute ★ = Close match — = No match

DMC	Royal Mouliné	Bates/ Anchor	DMC	Royal Mouliné	Bates/ Anchor	DMC	Royal Mouliné	Bates/ Anchor	DMC	Royal Mouliné	Bates/ Anchor	DMC	Royal Mouliné	Bates/ Anchor	DMC	Royal Mouliné	Bates/ Anchor
White	1001	2	437	8200★	362	680	6260★	901	816	2530	44★	936	5260T	269	3326	2115★	25★
Ecru	8600	926	444	6155★	291	699	5375	923★	817	2415T	19	937	5260	268	3328	2045	11★
208	3335★	110★	445	6000	288	700	5365★	229	818	2505★	48	938	8430	381	3340	—	329
209	3415★	105	451	—	399★	701	5365★	227	819	2000	892★	939	4405	127	3341	—	328
210	3320★	104	452	—	399★	702	5330	239	820	4345	134	943	4935★	188★	3345	5025T	268★
211	3410	108★	453	1015T	397★	703	5320	238	822	8605★	387★	945	8020★	347★	3346	5220T	257★
221	2570	897★	469	5255	267★	704	5310★	256★	823	4400★	150	946	7230★	332★	3347	5210★	266★
223	2555	894	470	5255★	267	712	8600★	387★	824	4225	164★	947	7255★	330★	3348	5270★	265
224	2545	893	471	5245	266★	718	3015★	88	825	4215	162★	948	8070	778★	3350	2220	42★
225	2540	892	472	5240	264★	720	—	326	826	4210	161★	950	8020T	4146	3354	2210	74★
300	8330	352★	498	2425T	20★	721	—	324★	827	4605	159★	951	8020T	366★	3362	—	862★
301	8315★	349★	500	5125	879★	722	—	323★	828	4850	158★	954	5455★	203★	3363	—	861★
304	2415★	47★	501	5120★	878	725	6215	306★	829	5825	906	955	5450	206★	3364	—	843★
307	6005★	289★	502	5110	876	726	6150★	295	830	5825★	889★	956	2170★	40★	3371	8435	382
309	2525★	42★	503	5105	875	727	6135	293	831	5825T	889★	957	2160T	40★	3607	—	87★
310	1002	403	504	5100	213★	729	6255	890	832	5815	907	958	—	187	3608	—	86
311	4275T	149★	517	—	169★	730	—	924★	833	5815★	874★	959	—	186	3609	—	85
312	—	147★	518	4860★	168★	731	—	281★	834	5810★	874	961	2515★	76★	3685	2335	70★
315	3130	896★	519	4855T	167★	732	5925T	281★	838	8425★	380	962	2515	76★	3687	2325	69★
316	3120	895★	520	—	862★	733	—	280★	839	8560	380★	963	2505	49★	3688	2320	66★
317	1030★	400★	522	—	859★	734	—	279★	840	8555	379★	964	—	185	3689	2310	49
318	1020★	399★	523	—	859★	738	8245★	942	841	8550	378★	966	5150★	214★	3705	—	35★
319	5025	246★	524	—	858★	739	8240★	885★	842	8505	376★	970	7040	316★	3706	—	28★
320	5015	216★	535	1115T	401★	740	7045	316★	844	1115T	401★	971	7045	316★	3708	—	26★
321	2415	47	543	8500	933★	741	6125	304	869	8720★	944★	972	6120★	298	48	9000★	1201★
322	—	978★	550	3380★	102★	742	6120	303	890	5025★	879★	973	6015	290	51	9014	1220
326	2530	59★	552	3370★	101	743	6210	297	891	2135	35★	975	8365	355★	52	9006	1208
327	3365★	101★	553	3360	98	744	6110★	301★	892	2130	28	976	8355	308★	53	—	—
333	—	119	554	3355★	96★	745	6105	300★	893	2125★	27	977	8350	307★	57	9002	1203
334	4250T	145	561	—	212★	746	6100	386★	894	2115T	26	986	5430	246★	61	9013T	1218★
335	2525T	42★	562	—	210★	747	4850	158★	895	5430★	246★	987	5020★	244★	62	9000T	1201★
336	4270★	149★	563	—	208★	754	8075	778★	898	8425★	360	988	5295T	243★	67	—	1211★
340	—	118	564	—	203★	758	8080	868	899	2515	27★	989	5405T	242★	69	—	1218★
341	—	117	580	5935	267★	760	2035	9★	900	7230★	333	991	5165T	189★	75	9002	1206★
347	2425★	13★	581	5925	266★	761	2030	8★	902	—	72★	992	4925★	187★	90	9012★	1217
349	2400	13	597	4860★	168★	762	1010★	397★	904	5295★	258★	993	4915★	186★	91	9008★	1211
350	2045T	11	598	4855★	167★	772	—	264★	905	5295	258★	995	4710	410	92	9011T	1216★
351	2015T	11★	600	2225★	59★	775	4600★	128★	906	5285★	256★	996	4700	433	93	9007★	1210★
352	2015	10★	601	2225★	78★	776	2110★	24★	907	5280★	255	3011	5525T	845★	94	9011★	1216
353	2020★	8★	602	2640★	77★	778	3110	968★	909	5370	229★	3012	5525★	844★	95	9006T	1208★
355	8095	5968	603	2720★	76★	780	8215★	310★	910	5370★	228★	3013	5515	842★	99	9005T	1207★
356	8090	5975★	604	2710	75★	781	8215	309★	911	5465★	205★	3021	—	382★	101	9009★	1213★
367	5020	216★	605	2155	50★	782	6230	308	912	5465	205	3022	—	8581★	102	—	1208★
368	5005★	240★	606	7260	335	783	6220★	307	913	5460★	209	3023	—	8581★	103	—	1210★
369	5005	213★	608	7255	333★	791	4165★	941★	915	3030	89★	3024	1100	900★	104	9012	1217
370	—	889★	610	5825T	889★	792	4155T	940	917	3020★	89★	3031	—	905★	105	9013★	1218
371	—	888★	611	5735T	898	793	4155	121	918	8330★	341★	3032	8620T	903★	106	9002T	1203★
372	—	887★	612	8815★	832	794	4145	120★	919	8095★	341★	3033	8610★	388★	107	9003	1204
400	8325★	351	613	5605★	956★	796	4340	133★	920	8060★	339★	3041	3215★	871	108	9014★	1220★
402	8305★	347★	632	8530	936★	797	4265★	132★	921	8060T	349★	3042	3205★	869	111	—	1218★
407	8005	882★	640	8625	903	798	4325	131★	922	8315T	324★	3045	6260T	373★	112	9003T	1204★
413	1025★	401	642	8620★	392	799	4250★	130★	924	4830T	851★	3046	5810	887★	113	9007★	1210★
414	1020★	400★	644	8800	830	800	4310	128	926	4820★	779★	3047	5805	886★	114	9010	1215
415	1015	398	645	1115	905★	801	8405	357★	927	4810T	849★	3051	5530T	846★	115	9004	1206
420	8720★	375★	646	1115★	8581	806	4870T	169★	928	1010T	900★	3052	5060★	859★	121	9007	1210
422	8710★	373★	647	1110	8581★	807	4860★	168★	930	4510	922★	3053	5055★	859★	122	9010T	1215★
433	8265	371★	648	1100★	900	809	4145★	130★	931	4505	921★	3064	8005★	914★	123	—	1213★
434	8215★	309	666	2405	46	813	4610★	160★	932	4500	920★	3072	4805★	397★	124	9007T	1210★
435	8210★	369★	676	6250	891	814	2340T	44★	934	5070T	862★	3078	6130	292★	125	9009	1213
436	8205	363★	677	—	886★	815	2530★	43	935	5225T	862★	3325	4200	159★	126	9006★	1208★

2

Wallhangings, Pictures and Bell Pulls

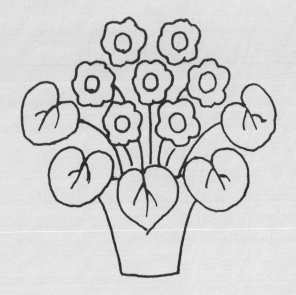

I know that nowadays nobody would come if you pulled the bell, but a bell pull
can be used purely for decoration and the length can be adjusted to the height of
your room. This is the advantage of repeat designs.

*Pictures do not have to be expensive. Why not embroider your favourite flower and
then frame it and hang it on the wall? If you don't want to spend too much money,
you can simply wrap the embroidery around a piece of thick cardboard and glue it
on the reverse side. It couldn't be simpler.*

WALLHANGING WITH ROSES

Material: linen, 10 threads per cm
(25 threads per in)
Cutting size: 20 × 65 cm
($7\frac{3}{4} \times 25\frac{1}{2}$ in)
Thread: DMC embroidery thread.
Use 2 strands in the needle
Interfacing

◨ 3345 very dark green

▨ 3346 dark green

☒ 470 medium green

◫ 471 light green

⊟ 580 dark yellowish green

◎ 581 light yellowish green

■ 347 very dark red

⊡ 891 dark red

▥ 351 medium red

L 3341 light red

◩ 353 very light red

⊡ 951 apricot

Fold the fabric in half lengthwise to
find the middle. Measure 5 cm (2 in)
from the top of the fabric and begin
to embroider at the arrow on the
graph. Press the finished embroidery.
Place the interfacing on the wrong
side of the work and fold the linen
over 3 threads from the motif. Sew it
down with small stitches. Make
casings at the top and bottom for the
fitting.

AFRICAN VIOLET

Material: linen, 10 threads per cm (25 threads per in)

Cutting size: 35 × 35 cm (13¾ × 13¾ in)

Finished size: 30 × 30 cm (11¾ × 11¾ in)

Thread: DMC embroidery floss. Use 2 strands in the needle

Stitch a green border (3347), 3 cm (1¼ in) from the flowers, and a row of backstitches in red (915). Cut a piece of white cardboard, press the embroidery and fold it round the card. Glue the edges onto the back.

■ 838 dark brown	◩ 3607 dark pink	L 3347 light green
◪ 839 medium brown	⊓ 3608 medium pink	◨ 580 dark yellowish green
☒ 840 light brown	⊡ 3609 light pink	⊠ 470 medium yellowish green
⊙ 315 reddish brown	⊙ 444 yellow	
◣ 915 dark red	▲ 3345 dark green	⊟ 471 light yellowish green
– 915 (backstitch)	⊟ 3346 medium green	⋀ 731 dull green

WALLHANGING: BUNCH OF WILD FLOWERS WITH CREEPING BELL FLOWER, SHRUBBY CINQUEFOIL AND CLOVER

Material: linen, 8 threads per cm (20 threads per in)
Cutting size: 35 × 45 cm ($13\frac{3}{4} × 17\frac{3}{4}$ in)
Finished size: 30 × 40 cm ($11\frac{3}{4} × 15\frac{3}{4}$ in)
A piece of thick cardboard: 30 × 40 cm ($11\frac{3}{4} × 15\frac{3}{4}$ in)
Thread: DMC embroidery floss. Use 3 strands in the needle

◣	895 dark green
◿	987 medium green
∧	989 light green
⊙	470 yellowish green
L	471 light yellowish green
◩	725 dark yellow
○	726 light yellow
S	333 dark blue
◪	340 medium blue
⊟	341 light blue
Ⅲ	3687 dark pink
）	3326 medium pink
∴	3689 light pink

Instructions for mounting are given on page 9.

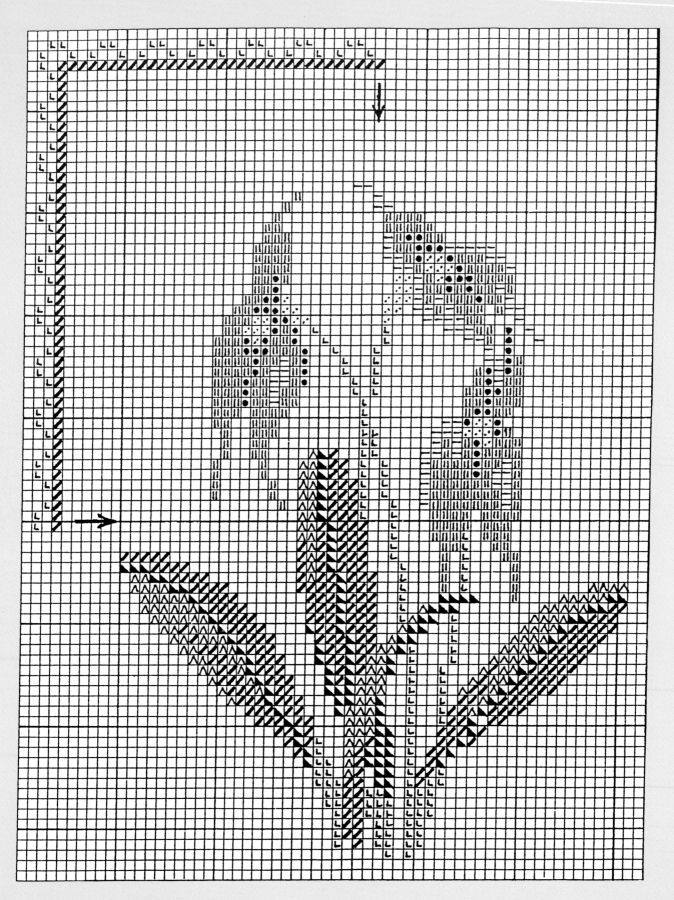

ORCHID
(*Masdevallia veitchiana*)

Material: linen, 10 threads per cm (25 threads per in)
Cutting size: 20 × 25 cm (7¾ × 9¾ in)
Finished size: 16 × 20 cm (6¼ × 7¾ in)
Thread: DMC embroidery floss. Use 2 strands in the needle

◣ 3345 dark green

◩ 905 medium green

⟨∧⟩ 906 light green

⊏ 907 very light green

⊡ 321 dark red

⫿ 350 light red

⊡ 962 pink

⊟ 947 orange

Fold the fabric, 11 threads from the border, over a piece of white cardboard and glue in place.

ORCHID
(*Phalaenopsis*)

Material: linen, 10 threads per cm
(25 threads per in)
Cutting size: 20 × 25 cm ($7\frac{3}{4} \times 9\frac{3}{4}$ in)
Finished size: 16 × 20 cm
($6\frac{1}{4} \times 7\frac{3}{4}$ in)
Thread: DMC embroidery floss. Use
2 strands in the needle

◪	905 medium green
⋀	906 light green
⌊	907 very light green
▲	730 dark dull green
⊚	3012 light dull green
⊟	971 orange
⊙	3328 dark rust
⊞	352 medium rust
·	948 light beige
◩	601 dark bluish red
⫿	603 medium bluish red
⫶	605 light bluish red

Fold the fabric, 11 threads from the
border, over a piece of white
cardboard and glue in place.

ORCHID – PINK
(*Cattleya*)

Material: linen, 10 threads per cm
(25 threads per in)
Cutting size: 20×25 cm ($7\frac{3}{4} \times 9\frac{3}{4}$ in)
Finished size: 16×20 cm
($6\frac{1}{4} \times 7\frac{3}{4}$ in)
Thread: DMC embroidery floss. Use
2 strands in the needle

◣   3345 dark green

◪   905 medium green

◮   906 light green

⌊   907 very light green

▥   680 brown

⊞   741 orange

◉   915 very dark cyclamen

◳   601 dark cyclamen

⌋   603 medium cyclamen

⊟   604 light cyclamen

⊡   818 very light cyclamen

Fold the fabric, 11 threads from the
border, over a piece of white
cardboard and glue in place.

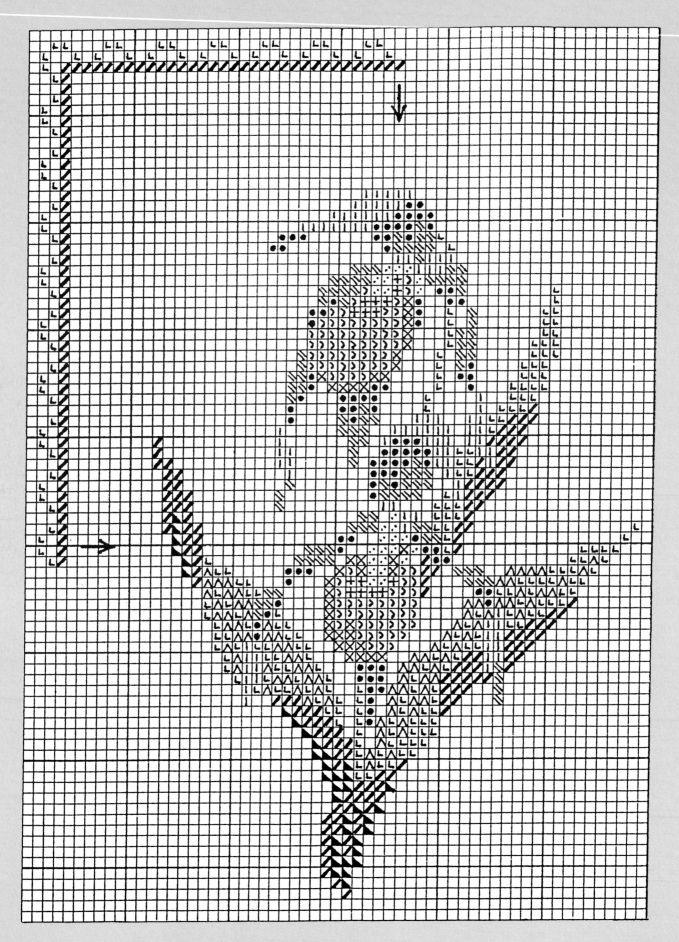

ORCHID
(*Cypripedium calceolus*)

Material: linen, 10 threads per cm
(25 threads per in)
Cutting size: 20×25 cm ($7\frac{3}{4} \times 9\frac{3}{4}$ in)
Finished size: 16×20 cm
($6\frac{1}{4} \times 7\frac{3}{4}$ in)
Thread: DMC embroidery floss. Use
2 strands in the needle

◥ 3345 dark green

◪ 905 medium green

⌃ 906 light green

ᴸ 907 very light green

⊞ 734 dull green

⊙ 632 brown

◩ 301 rust

Ⅱ 436 light rust

⊠ 725 dark yellow

⟩ 973 medium yellow

⋅ 3078 light yellow

Fold the fabric, 11 threads from the
border, over a piece of white
cardboard and glue in place.

ORCHID – YELLOW
(*Cattleya*)

Material: linen, 10 threads per cm
(25 threads per in)
Cutting size: 20 × 25 cm (7¾ × 9¾ in)
Finished size: 16 × 20 cm
(6¼ × 7¾ in)
Thread: DMC embroidery floss. Use
2 strands in the needle

◣ 3345 dark green

◪ 905 medium green

⊿ 906 light green

ʟ 907 very light green

⊙ 734 light dull green

● 891 red

⊠ 603 dark pink

Ⅱ 776 light pink

⊟ 741 dark orange

◨ 742 light orange

) 743 yellow

⋅ 726 light yellow

Fold the fabric, 11 threads from the
border, over a piece of white
cardboard and glue in place.

ORCHID
(*Vanda coerulea*)

Material: linen, 10 threads per cm
(25 threads per in)
Cutting size: 20×25 cm ($7\frac{3}{4} \times 9\frac{3}{4}$ in)
Finished size: 16×20 cm
($6\frac{1}{4} \times 7\frac{3}{4}$ in)
Thread: DMC embroidery floss. Use
2 strands in the needle

◣ 3345 dark green

◪ 905 medium green

⌃ 906 light green

L 907 very light green

◎ 734 light dull green

· 743 yellow

● 333 dark blue

‖ 340 medium blue

+ 341 light blue

◺ 211 light lilac

Fold the fabric, 11 threads from the
border, over a piece of white
cardboard and glue in place.

FRAMED PANSIES

Material: linen, 10 threads per cm
(25 threads per in)
Cutting size: 18 × 22 cm (7 × 9 in)
Frame (inside): 12 × 17 cm
($4\frac{3}{4} \times 6\frac{3}{4}$ in)
Thread: DMC embroidery floss. Use
2 strands in the needle

◪	987 dark green
‖	906 medium green
∧	907 light green
◎	734 light yellowish green
●	333 dark blue
⊞	340 light blue
◥	3021 dark brown
Ⓢ	741 orange
⋅	3078 light yellow
⊟	347 dark red
⊠	3328 medium red
L	352 light red

Iron the finished embroidery and fit
into the frame.

3

Placemats and Plate Liners

*M*ost dining-tables are rectangular to make it easy to lay the table but the
designs shown on the next few pages can easily be adapted for oval or round shapes.
In such cases you just have to edge the embroidery with bias binding in a suitable
colour, with lace or with broderie anglaise instead of fringes or embroidered borders.
If you wish to make personalized plate liners a monogram is just the thing.
Further on in the book you can find styles for the whole alphabet.

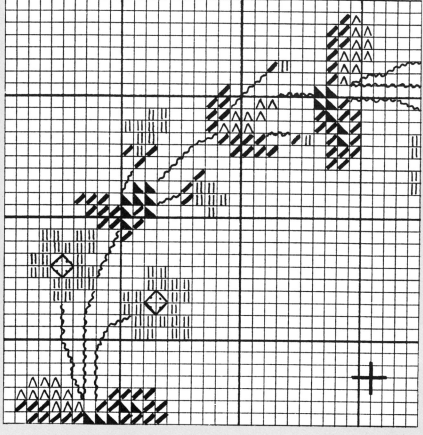

PLATE LINER WITH SCARLET PIMPERNEL

Material: linen, 10 threads per cm
(25 threads per in)
Cutting size: 20 × 20 cm (7¾ × 7¾ in)
Finished size: 15 × 15 cm (6 × 6 in)
Lace: 50 cm (19¾ in)
Thread: DMC embroidery floss. Use
2 strands in the needle

—	221 reddish brown (backstitch)
▥	608 red
·	445 yellow
◣	3346 dark green
◪	3347 medium green
~	3347 (backstitch)
∧	471 light green

Make a small hem about 0.75 cm
(¼ in) from the embroidery, pin lace
around and machine-stitch.

PLATE LINER WITH BIRD'S FOOT TREFOIL

Material: linen, 10 threads per cm
(25 threads per in)
Cutting size: 20 × 20 cm (7¾ × 7¾ in)
Finished size: 15 × 15 cm (6 × 6 in)
Lace: 50 cm (19¾ in)
Thread: DMC embroidery floss. Use
2 strands in the needle

◣ 3346 dark green

◪ 470 medium green

∧ 471 light green

~ 407 reddish beige (backstitch)

● 971 orange

‖ 972 dark yellow

L 973 light yellow

Hem as for Plate Liner with Scarlet
Pimpernel, page 35.

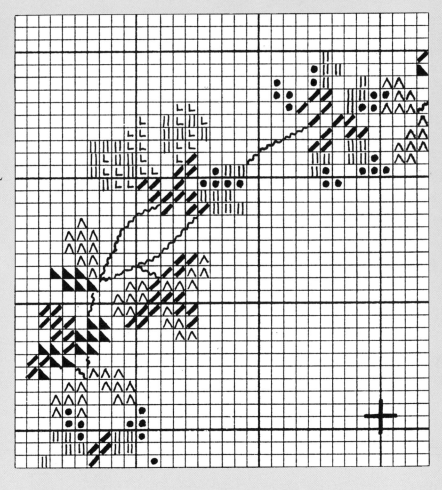

PLATE LINER
WITH SPEEDWELL

Material: linen, 10 threads per cm
(25 threads per in)
Cutting size: 20×20 cm ($7\frac{3}{4} \times 7\frac{3}{4}$ in)
Finished size: 15×15 cm (6×6 in)
Lace: 50 cm ($19\frac{3}{4}$ in)
Thread: DMC embroidery floss. Use
2 strands in the needle

⊙	798 dark blue
‖	799 medium blue
L	341 light blue
~	407 reddish beige (backstitch)
◣	3346 dark green
◿	3347 medium green
∧	471 light green
·	white
····	white (backstitch)

Hem as for Plate Liner with Scarlet
Pimpernel, page 35.

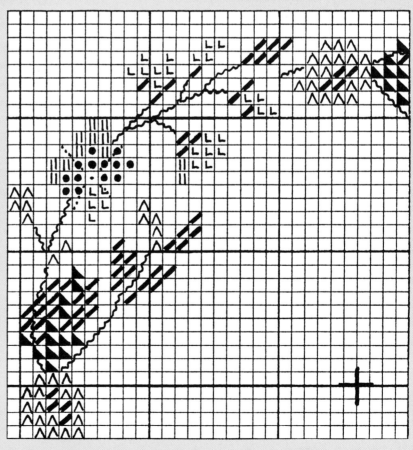

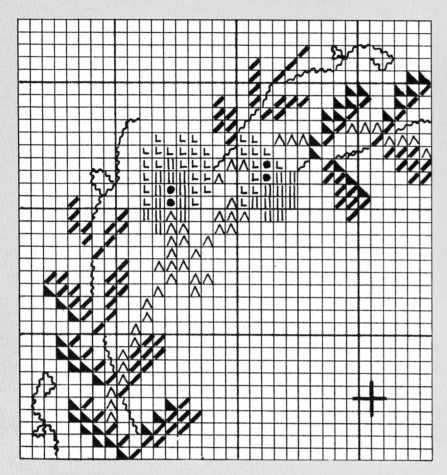

PLATE LINER WITH VETCH

Material: linen, 10 threads per cm
(25 threads per in)
Cutting size: 20 × 20 cm (7¾ × 7¾ in)
Finished size: 15 × 15 cm (6 × 6 in)
Lace: 50 cm (19¾ in)
Thread: DMC embroidery floss. Use
2 strands in the needle

◤ 3346 dark green

◪ 3347 medium green

~ 3347 (backstitch)

∧ 471 light green

• 552 dark lilac

⫼ 553 medium lilac

L 3608 light lilac

Hem as for Plate Liner with Scarlet
Pimpernel, page 35.

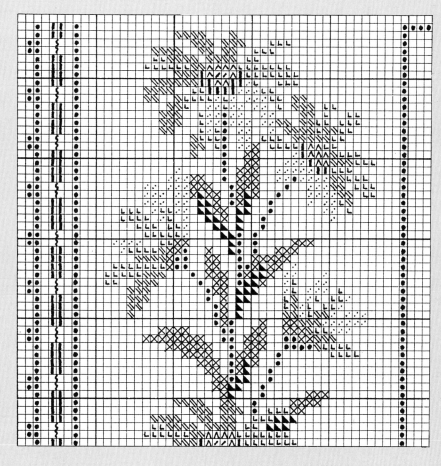

PLACEMAT WITH CHRYSANTHEMUMS

Material: linen, 10 threads per cm (25 threads per in)
Cutting size: 45 × 35 cm ($17\frac{3}{4}$ × $13\frac{3}{4}$ in)
Finished size: 40 × 30 cm ($15\frac{3}{4}$ × $11\frac{3}{4}$ in)
Lace: 65 cm ($25\frac{1}{2}$ in)
Thread: DMC embroidery floss. Use 2 strands in the needle

●	733 yellowish green
◣	3346 dark green
☒	581 medium green
~	581 (backstitch)
▯	680 light brown
⌃	729 golden
⧄	444 yellow
⧅	891 red
L	893 pink
⸬	3708 light pink

Make a 1-cm ($\frac{1}{2}$-in) hem for the short ends and a 0.75-cm ($\frac{1}{4}$-in) hem along each long edge. Machine-stitch the lace for the short edges.

PLATE LINER

Cutting size: 20 × 20 cm ($7\frac{3}{4}$ × $7\frac{3}{4}$ in)
Finished size: 14 × 14 cm ($5\frac{1}{2}$ × $5\frac{1}{2}$ in) + lace.
Lace: 80 cm ($31\frac{1}{2}$ in)

Make a 0.75-cm ($\frac{1}{4}$-in) hem all round.

PLACEMAT WITH POINSETTIA

Material: linen, 10 threads per cm (25 threads per in)
Cutting size: 38 × 48 cm (15 × 19 in)
Finished size: 34 × 48 cm ($13\frac{1}{2}$ × 19 in)
Thread: DMC embroidery floss. Use 2 strands in the needle

◣ 987 dark green

◪ 989 medium green

⊠ 471 light green

⊡ 309 dark pink

⧈ 893 medium pink

⊞ 894 light pink

⊓ 776 very light pink

◼ 434 brown

ᒪ 307 yellow

Begin to embroider the border 3 cm ($1\frac{1}{4}$ in) from the top and 2 cm ($\frac{3}{4}$ in) from the left-hand edge. Make a 9-thread hem on the long sides and, on the short sides, make a line of machine-stitching 5 threads from the border and fray the remaining 1.5 cm ($\frac{5}{8}$ in).

PLACEMAT WITH TULIP

Material: linen, 10 threads per cm
(25 threads per in)
Cutting size: 38 × 48 cm (15 × 19 in)
Finished size: 34 × 48 cm
(13½ × 19 in)
Thread: DMC embroidery floss. Use
2 strands in the needle

◤ 987 dark green

◪ 989 medium green

⊠ 471 light green

⊙ 309 dark pink

◩ 893 medium pink

⊞ 894 light pink

⊓ 776 very light pink

Begin to embroider the border 3 cm
(1¼ in) from the top and 2 cm (¾ in)
from the left-hand edge. Make a 9-
thread hem on the long sides and, on
the short sides, make a line of
machine-stitching 5 threads from the
border and fray the remaining 1.5 cm
(⅝ in).

PLACEMAT WITH LILY

Material: linen, 10 threads per cm
(25 threads per in)
Cutting size: 38 × 48 cm (15 × 19 in)
Finished size: 34 × 48 cm
($13\frac{1}{2}$ × 19 in)
Thread: DMC embroidery floss. Use
2 strands in the needle

◥ 987 dark green

◪ 989 medium green

⊠ 471 light green

⊡ 472 very light green

⊙ 309 dark pink

◩ 893 medium pink

⊞ 894 light pink

◫ 776 very light pink

◼ 434 brown

Begin to embroider the border 3 cm
($1\frac{1}{4}$ in) from the top and 2 cm ($\frac{3}{4}$ in)
from the left-hand edge. Make a 9–
thread hem on the long sides and, on
the short sides, make a line of
machine-stitching 5 threads from the
border and fray the remaining 1.5 cm
($\frac{5}{8}$ in).

Placemat with dahlia

Material: linen, 10 threads per cm
(25 threads per in)
Cutting size: 38 × 48 cm (15 × 19 in)
Finished size: 34 × 48 cm
(13½ × 19 in)
Thread: DMC embroidery floss. Use
2 strands in the needle

◣ 987 dark green

◪ 989 medium green

☒ 471 light green

◉ 309 dark pink

◨ 893 medium pink

⊞ 894 light pink

⊓ 776 very light pink

◉ 727 yellow

Begin to embroider the border 3 cm
(1¼ in) from the top and 2 cm (¾ in)
from the left-hand edge. Make a 9-
thread hem on the long sides and, on
the short sides, make a line of
machine-stitching 5 threads from the
border and fray the remaining 1.5 cm
(⅝ in).

Plate liner with 'A' monogram

Material: linen, 10 threads per cm
(25 threads per in)
Cutting size: 20×20 cm ($7\frac{3}{4} \times 7\frac{3}{4}$ in)
Finished size: 15×15 cm (6×6 in)
Thread: DMC embroidery floss. Use
2 strands in the needle

- ■ 936 dark green
- ◣ 3346 medium green
- ▨ 581 light green
- ⊠ 783 golden (+monogram)
- ⊡ 743 yellow
- ◪ 917 dark cyclamen
- ⋀ 3607 light cyclamen
- ⦿ 552 dark lilac
- ⦀ 553 medium lilac
- ⊟ 554 light lilac

To hem, fold over 5 and then 9
threads to the wrong side and sew a
hemstitch border over 2 threads with
581.

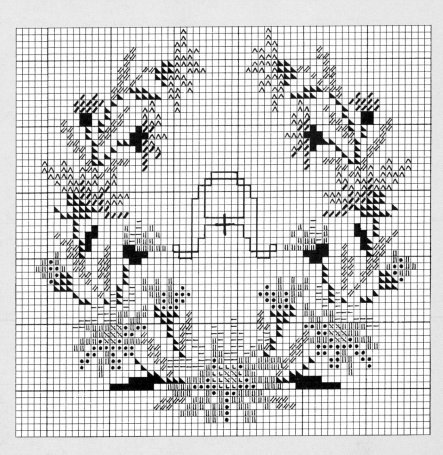

Material: linen, 10 threads per cm
(25 threads per in)
Cutting size: 20 × 20 cm (7¾ × 7¾ in)
Finished size: 15 × 15 cm (6 × 6 in)
Thread: DMC embroidery floss. Use
2 strands in the needle

◥ 3346 dark green

▨ 581 medium green

◳ 471 light green

● 309 red

△ 3688 dark pink

⊓ 3689 light pink

   451 grey (monogram)

Hemstitch as before, using 471.

Plate liner with 'B' monogram

PLATE LINER WITH 'C' MONOGRAM

Material: linen, 10 threads per cm (25 threads per in)
Cutting size: 20 × 20 cm (7¾ × 7¾ in)
Finished size: 15 × 15 cm (6 × 6 in)
Thread: DMC embroidery floss. Use 2 strands in the needle

◥ 3346 dark green

~ 3346 (backstitch)

▨ 581 medium green

◲ 471 light green

● 333 dark blue

⋀ 340 medium blue

⫿ 341 light blue

783 golden (monogram)

Hemstitch as before, using 471.

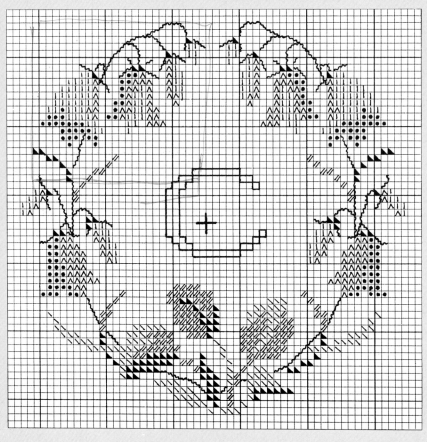

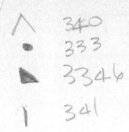

340
333
3346
341

Thread: DMC embroidery floss. Use
2 strands in the needle

- ■ 936 very dark green
- ◣ 3346 dark green
- ▨ 581 medium green
  (+ monogram)
- ◲ 471 light green
- ⊙ 917 dark pink
- ⋀ 3607 medium pink
- ⊓ 957 light pink
- ⊡ 743 yellow

Hemstitch as before, using 471.

PLATE LINER WITH 'E' MONOGRAM

Material: linen, 10 threads per cm (25 threads per in)
Cutting size: 20×20 cm ($7\frac{3}{4} \times 7\frac{3}{4}$ in)
Finished size: 15×15 cm (6×6 in)
Thread: DMC embroidery floss. Use 2 strands in the needle

- ◣ 3346 dark green
- ◪ 581 medium green
- ● 407 reddish beige (+monogram)
- ···· 407 (backstitch)
- ⊞ 353 medium reddish beige
- ◺ 948 light beige
- ⊟ 891 red
- ◹ 893 dark pink
- ☐ 957 light pink

Hemstitch as before, using 581.

PLACEMAT

Material: linen, 10 threads per cm (25 threads per in)
Cutting size: 40×50 cm ($15\frac{3}{4} \times 19\frac{3}{4}$ in)
Finished size: 35×45 cm ($13\frac{3}{4} \times 17\frac{3}{4}$ in)

- ◣ 3346 dark green
- ◪ 581 light green

Begin to embroider the border 2.5 cm (1 in) from the edges. To hem, fold over 5 and then 9 threads to the wrong side.

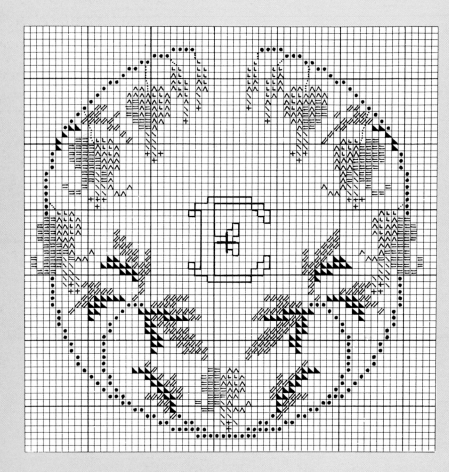

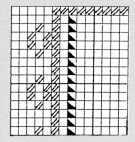

Plate liner with 'F' monogram

Material: linen, 10 threads per cm
(25 threads per in)
Cutting size: 20 × 20 cm (7¾ × 7¾ in)
Finished size: 15 × 15 cm (6 × 6 in)
Thread: DMC embroidery floss. Use
2 strands in the needle

◥ 3346 dark green

▨ 581 medium green

~ 581 (backstitch)

◩ 471 light green

● 333 dark blue

▵ 340 medium blue

Ⅱ 341 light blue

783 golden (monogram)

Hemstitch as before, using 471.

4

Samplers

O*n page 56 you will find a suggestion for a sampler with only two colours. Of course, if you want to make it more colourful, you can easily do so by adding just as many colours as you want.*

On page 58 you will find the whole alphabet. If you want to make your own personal sampler, and I know that lots of people do, simply choose from the flower designs in this book and frame them with one of the many border ideas. The two wreaths can be used for a name or other information.

Material: Aida, $4\frac{1}{2}$ stitches per cm
(11 stitches per in)
Cutting size: 20×18 cm ($7\frac{3}{4} \times 7$ in)
Finished size: 15×13.5 cm
($6 \times 5\frac{1}{4}$ in) (You will need a piece of
cardboard in the same size.)
Thread: DMC embroidery floss. Use
3 strands in the needle

- ● 731 dark dull green
- ▨ 734 light dull green
- ◣ 906 green
- ▧ 907 light green
- ⋀ 444 yellow
- Ⅼ 307 light yellow
- ■ 920 rust

Press the finished embroidery. With
the embroidered side face down, lay
the cardboard in the centre of the
wrong side and turn the edges of the
fabric under. Glue them to the
cardboard.

Wreath of forsythia

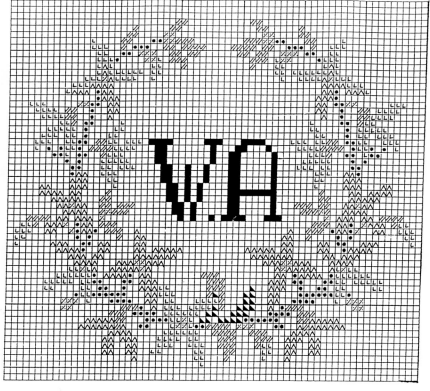

WREATH OF FLOWERS

Material: Aida, $4\frac{1}{2}$ stitches per cm (11 stitches per in)
Cutting size: 21 × 14 cm ($8\frac{1}{4}$ × $5\frac{1}{2}$ in)
Finished size: 17.5 × 10 cm (7 × 4 in)
(You will need a piece of cardboard in the same size.)
Thread: DMC embroidery floss. Use 3 strands in the needle

- ⦿ 733 dull green
- – 733 (backstitch)
- ◣ 906 green
- ▨ 907 light green
- ⋀ 48 pink (shaded colour)
- ⸬ 307 yellow
- – 208 lilac (backstitch for name)

Press the finished embroidery. With the embroidered side face down, lay the cardboard in the centre of the wrong side and turn the edges of the fabric under. Glue them to the cardboard.

CHILD'S SAMPLER

Material: linen, 10 threads per cm (25 threads per in)
Cutting size: 30 × 42 cm ($11\frac{3}{4}$ × $16\frac{1}{2}$ in)
Finished size: 26 × 36 cm ($10\frac{1}{4}$ × $14\frac{1}{4}$ in)
Thread: DMC embroidery floss. Use 2 strands in the needle

- ◣ 797 blue
- – 797 (backstitch)
- ⋀ 518 turquoise

Place a piece of interfacing on top of the wrong side, turn the edges of the linen to the back at the long sides and sew with small stitches. Then make a casing at the top and bottom edges and insert a brass or bamboo fitting.

ALPHABETS

5

Tablecloths

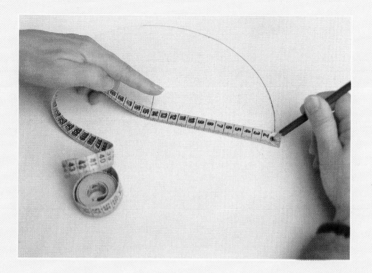

*E*mbroidered tablecloths are not the most practical things, and you will simply
have to smile graciously if guests spill red wine or sauce on the cloth.
But hand-embroidered table linen looks beautiful.

The material I chose for the rose cloth is specially woven, but there are many
similar ones you can buy in the shops. I think it is more practical to embroider a
table centre and put it on a plain or white cloth which can stand any amount of
washing. In the photograph you can see how easy it is to draw a circle. Be careful
when you choose the fabric. The embroidery material must have the same density of
thread in height and width, or the result will be oval instead of round!

CLOTH WITH ROSES

Material: special texture, a square with room for at least 49 stitches and with about 5 stitches per cm (13 stitches per in)
Cutting size: 150 × 150 cm (60 × 60 in)
Thread: DMC embroidery floss. Use 2 strands in the needle

■ 451 grey (about 4 skeins)

◨ 580 dark green (2 skeins)

⊠ 581 medium green (3 skeins)

⊟ 472 light green (1 skein)

◣ 347 dark red (1 skein)

▨ 350 medium red (2 skeins)

△ 3706 light red (2 skeins)

Ⅲ 776 very light red (1 skein)

Finish the cloth with a 1.5-cm ($\frac{5}{8}$-in) fringe.

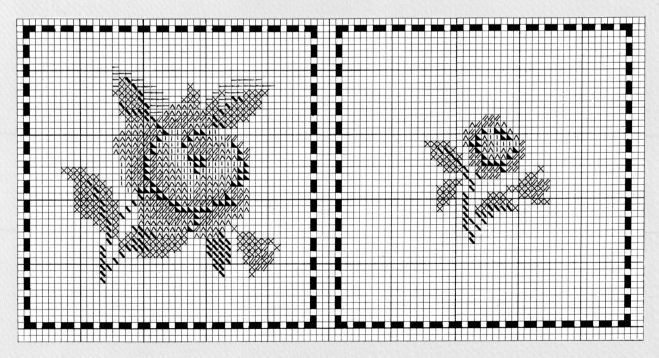

DOILY WITH PRIMROSES

Material: Aida, $5\frac{1}{2}$ stitches per cm
($13\frac{1}{2}$ stitches per inch)
Cutting size: 26×26 cm
($10\frac{1}{4} \times 10\frac{1}{4}$ in)
Finished size: 21×21 cm
($8\frac{1}{4} \times 8\frac{1}{4}$ in)
Edging: 1 m ($39\frac{1}{2}$ in)
Thread: DMC embroidery floss. Use
2 strands in the needle

◣ 469 dark green

◪ 581 medium green

ᴸ 471 light green

◉ 601 dark red

⊼ 603 light red

◺ 725 dark yellow

⋰ 726 light yellow

Turn up hem and stitch in place. Pin
edging around and machine-stitch.

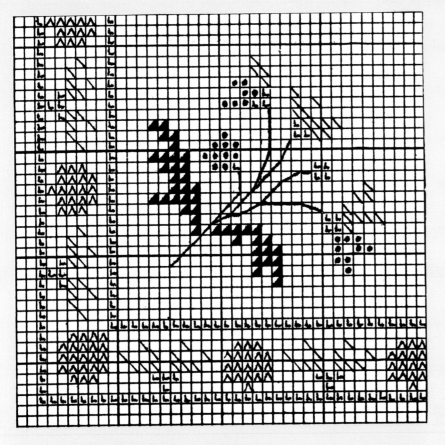

DOILY WITH STYLIZED FLOWERS

Material: Aida, $5\frac{1}{2}$ stitches per cm ($13\frac{1}{2}$ stitches per inch)
Cutting size: 28 × 28 cm (11 × 11 in)
Thread: DMC embroidery floss. Use 2 strands in the needle

- ◪ 988 dark green
- ∧ 989 light green
- L 581 yellowish green
- – 581 (backstitch)
- ● 893 dark pink
- ◺ 604 light pink

Press the finished embroidery. Two threads from the outermost row, machine-stitch around the doily. Fray the fabric to make a fringe 1.5 cm ($\frac{5}{8}$ in) deep.

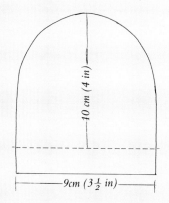

EGG COSIES

Material: (2 pieces) 11 × 12 cm
($4\frac{1}{2} \times 4\frac{3}{4}$ in)

With right sides facing, sew around
both pieces of fabric, leaving the
bottom open. Turn bottom edge to
wrong side for hem and sew or glue
in place. Turn to right side. Sew or
glue braid over seam.

TABLE MAT WITH FLORAL BORDER

Material: beige Aida, $4\frac{1}{2}$ stitches per
cm (11 stitches per in)
Cutting size: 40 × 40 cm
($15\frac{3}{4} \times 15\frac{3}{4}$ in)
Finished size: 34 × 34 cm
($13\frac{1}{2} \times 13\frac{1}{2}$ in)
Thread: DMC embroidery floss. Use
3 strands in the needle

- ☒ 906 dark green (2 skeins)
- ~ 906 (backstitch)
- Ⅱ 907 light green
- ⊙ 340 dark blue
- L 341 light blue
- ■ 783 golden
- — 783 (backstitch)

Turn a 1-cm ($\frac{1}{2}$-in) hem under on all
edges and sew in place. Press on
wrong side of embroidery.

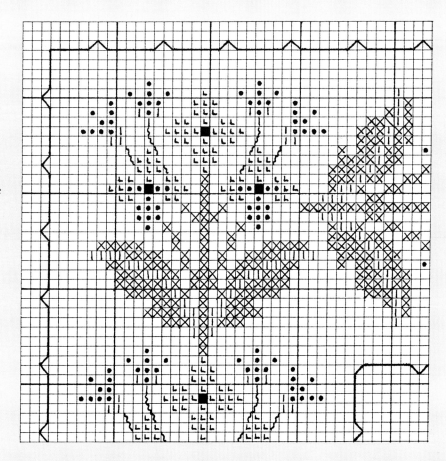

WREATH WITH FIELD FLOWERS

Material: Aida, 5½ stitches per cm (13½ stitches per inch)
Cutting size: 35 × 35 cm (13¾ × 13¾ in)
Finished size: as above.
Bias binding: 110 cm (43 in)
Thread: DMC embroidery floss. Use 2 strands in the needle

Cut the fabric 3 cm (1¼ in) from the embroidery, pin the bias binding around and machine-stitch.

◣ 986 dark green
☒ 988 light green
− 988 (backstitch)
◿ 469 dark yellowish green
⋀ 581 light yellowish green
⋯ 581 (backstitch)
◺ 725 dark yellow

ㄴ 973 light yellow
● 603 dark pink
◺ 604 light pink
∥ 208 dark lilac
○ 209 medium lilac
⊟ 210 light lilac

TABLE CENTRE WITH TULIPS AND CHIONODOXA

Material: linen, 10 threads per cm (25 threads per in)
Cutting size: 50 × 50 cm ($19\frac{3}{4} \times 19\frac{3}{4}$ in)
Finished size: 47 × 47 cm ($18\frac{1}{2} \times 18\frac{1}{2}$ in)
Bias tape: 150 cm (60 in)
Thread: DMC embroidery floss. Use 2 strands in the needle

- 309 dark pink
- 962 medium pink (2 skeins)
- 894 light pink (2 skeins)
- 776 very light rose
- 987 dark green
- 988 medium green
- 989 light green
- 471 very light green
- 3371 very dark brown
- 840 medium brown (backstitch)
- 793 dark blue
- 341 light blue
- 3047 light yellow

Cut the fabric 1.5 cm ($\frac{5}{8}$ in) from the border, pin the bias binding around and machine stitch.

Material: linen, 10 threads per cm
(25 threads per in)
Cutting size: 38 × 38 cm (15 × 15 in)
Finished size: 34 × 34 cm
(13½ × 13½ in)
Lace: 115 cm (45 in)
Thread: DMC embroidery floss. Use
2 strands in the needle

- ◣ 986 dark green
- ◪ 3346 medium green
- ⊠ 3347 light green
- ⊡ 471 very light green
- ◩ 734 light yellowish green
- ⊙ 304 dark red
- ⫴ 891 light red

- ⊞ 893 dark pink
- Ⓢ 760 medium pink
- ◿ 754 light pink
- − 754 (backstitch)
- ■ 632 brown
- ∧ 301 medium brown
- ⊙ 402 light brown

CLOTH WITH HONEYSUCKLE

6

Cushions

The patterns for cushions shown on the following pages can be used for many other items, such as chair seats or footstools. Use wool instead of floss, if you decide to cover a footstool. Choose a suitable colour as the background, and canvas instead of linen. This will give the embroidery a much longer life.

CUSHION
WITH TULIPS

Material: beige Aida, $4\frac{1}{2}$ stitches per cm (11 stitches per in)
Cutting size: 45×45 cm ($17\frac{3}{4} \times 17\frac{3}{4}$ in)
Thread: DMC embroidery floss. Use 3 strands in the needle

◣ 832 light golden brown

◪ 734 light yellowish green

● 350 red

∧ 893 dark pink

L 604 light pink

⊟ 470 dark green

◸ 471 light green

– 471 (backstitch)

Iron the finished embroidery. Cut a piece of linen for the back the same size as the front. Place both sides together, right sides facing, with pre-gathered ruffling in between. Machine-stitch, leaving the bottom side open for a zipper of about 30 cm ($11\frac{3}{4}$ in). Insert pillow.

CUSHION
WITH CHRYSANTHEMUMS

Material: white Aida, $5\frac{1}{2}$ stitches per cm ($13\frac{1}{2}$ stitches per in)
Cutting size: (2 pieces) 42×38 cm ($16\frac{1}{2} \times 15$ in)
Finished size: 38×34 cm ($15 \times 13\frac{1}{2}$ in)
Edging: 250 cm ($98\frac{1}{2}$ in)
Thread: DMC embroidery floss. Use 2 strands in the needle

- ◉ 733 yellowish green
- ◣ 3346 dark green
- ⊠ 581 medium green
- ~ 581 (backstitch)

- ⫘ 680 light brown
- ⋀ 729 golden
- ◧ 741 dark orange
- ⌷ 972 medium orange
- ⋰ 444 yellow

Iron the finished embroidery. Cut a piece of linen for the back the same size as the front. Place both sides together, right sides facing, with pre-gathered ruffling in between. Machine-stitch, leaving the bottom side open for a zipper of about 30 cm ($11\frac{3}{4}$ in). Insert pad.

CUSHION WITH BUNCHES OF BLUEBELLS AND PRIMULAS

Material: Aida, $4\frac{1}{2}$ stitches per cm (11 stitches per in)
Cutting size: (2 pieces) 40 × 40 cm ($15\frac{3}{4}$ × $15\frac{3}{4}$ in)
Zipper: 30 cm ($11\frac{3}{4}$ in)
Thread: DMC embroidery floss. Use 3 strands in the needle

◣ 986 dark green

◥ 988 light green

~ 988 (backstitch)

∧ 581 yellowish green

··· 581 (backstitch)

⊙ 444 yellow

✕ 603 dark pink

𝕀 604 light pink

╱ 209 blue

L 210 light blue

Iron the finished embroidery. Cut a piece of linen for the back the same size as the front. Place both sides together, right sides facing, with pre-gathered ruffling in between. Machine-stitch, leaving the bottom side open for a zipper of about 30 cm ($11\frac{3}{4}$ in). Insert pad.

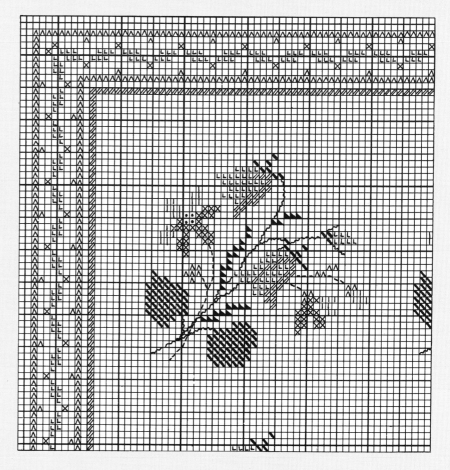

CUSHION WITH WATER-LILY

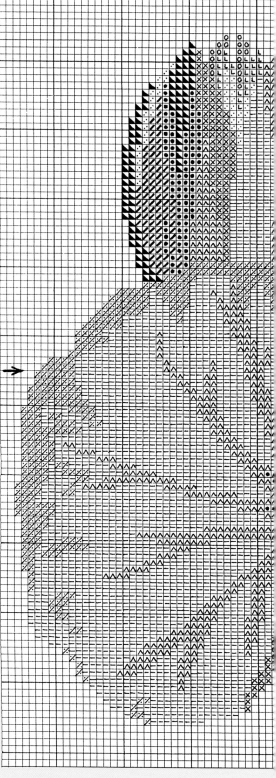

Material: beige linen, 10 threads per cm (25 threads per in)

Cutting size: 40 × 45 cm (15¾ × 17¾ in)

Finished size: about 34 × 40 cm (13½ × 15¾ in)

Cord: about 2 m (79 in)

Zipper: 30 cm (11¾ in)

Thread: DMC embroidery floss. Use 2 strands in the needle

Find the centre of the design and of the material and begin to embroider from there. Iron the finished embroidery and stitch, right sides together, leaving the bottom open for the zipper. Insert zipper and stitch cord around seam.

◥	895 very dark green
▯	904 dark green
◨	3346 medium green
⋀	470 light green
●	580 dark yellowish green

- 581 light yellowish green
- 730 dark dull green
- 732 medium dull green
- 734 light dull green
- 833 light golden
- 782 copper
- 738 beige
- 739 light beige
- 973 yellow
- 742 orange
- 893 dark pink
- 957 medium pink
- 776 light pink
- white

CUSHION WITH TULIPS

Material: linen, 8 threads per cm
(20 threads per in)
Cutting size: 42 × 42 cm
(16½ × 16½ in)
Finished size: 37 × 37 cm
(14½ × 14½ in)
Cord: 110 cm (43 in)
Zipper: 30 cm (11¾ in).
Thread: DMC embroidery floss. Use
3 strands in the needle

◣ 904 dark green

◪ 906 medium green

⋀ 907 light green

— 472 very light green (backstitch)

Ⅱ 721 dark orange

✕ 741 medium orange

⊟ 742 light orange

⋅ 973 yellow

⊟ 333 dark blue

⊞ 340 light blue

◧ 732 dull green

■ 3371 very dark brown

● 632 dark brown

◩ 840 medium brown

Ⅽ 841 light brown

Find the centre of the design and of
the material and begin to embroider
from there. Mark a circular outline,
diameter 38 cm (15 in), and fill the
background with backstitch,
following the chart.

SEAT-COVER WITH VIBURNUM

Material: beige Aida, 5 stitches per cm (13 stitches per in)
Thread: DMC embroidery floss. Use 3 strands in the needle

☑ 986 dark green

⊟ 3346 medium green

– 3346 (backstitch)

☒ 3347 light green

L 368 very light green

◣ 610 brown

⌃ 224 pink

Ⅱ 818 light pink

⋅ 744 light yellow

⊙ 400 reddish brown

Ⅲ 3328 red

■ 310 black

Place a sheet of paper over your chair and draw the outline of the seat, leaving 2 cm (¾ in) extra for seam and shrinkage allowance. Place the pattern on the linen and baste along the outline. Find the centre of the fabric and of the graph and begin from there.

   When you have finished, cut the top and back of the seat cushion according to the paper pattern. Place foam rubber or other washable padding between the two layers and stitch them together.

CUSHION WITH STYLIZED FLOWERS

Material: linen, 8 threads per cm
(20 threads per in)
Cutting size: 40 × 36 cm
($15\frac{3}{4} \times 14\frac{1}{4}$ in)
Finished size: 36 × 32 cm
($14\frac{1}{4} \times 12\frac{1}{2}$ in)
Cord: 140 cm (55 in)
Thread: DMC embroidery floss. Use
3 strands in the needle

⊠   989 green

–   989 (backstitch)

◣   610 brown

◿   841 light brown

▥   734 golden

◉   3688 pink

····   3688 (backstitch)

⬚   727 yellow

Iron the finished embroidery. Cut a
piece of linen for the back the same
size as the front. Place both sides
together, right sides facing, and stitch
leaving the bottom side open for the
zipper: about 30 cm ($11\frac{3}{4}$ in). Stitch
cord around seam on all four sides.
Fill with pad the appropriate size.

7

Variations on a Theme

*H*ere is an example of how you can adapt the same design for various useful
and decorative purposes. You can limit yourself to small ideas, for instance
bookmarks, which can be made very quickly, or you can undertake more ambitious
projects such as tea cosies or curtains. I have used stylized flowers, so you are free
to choose colours which match your décor or your personal taste.

VIOLETS

Material: linen with 10 threads per cm (25 threads per in).
Cutting size: the book's surface +5 cm (2 in) depth and +20 cm (7¾ in) for the flap
Thread: DMC embroidery floss. Use 2 strands in the needle

- ■ 552 dark lilac
- ◪ 553 medium lilac
- ▥ 554 light lilac
- ⊙ 741 orange
- ◨ 3345 very dark green
- ◉ 3346 dark green
- ⊠ 989 medium green
- ⊡ 471 light green
- ◺ 834 light golden

BOOK-COVER

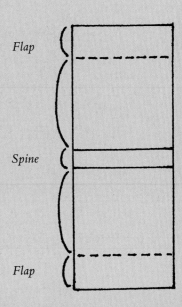

Flap

Spine

Flap

SHELF BORDER

Material: linen, 10 threads per cm
(25 threads per in)
Cutting size: 13 cm (5 in) × length
of your shelf
Finished size: 5.5 cm (2¼ in) deep
Thread: DMC embroidery floss. Use
2 strands in the needle

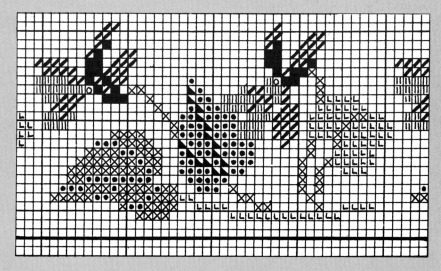

■	552 dark lilac	◥	3345 very dark green
▨	553 medium lilac	●	3346 dark green
⦀	554 light lilac	☒	989 medium green
⊙	741 orange	L	471 light green
–	741 (backstitch)		

SET OF FOUR DESIGNS

WALL ORNAMENT
Material: beige Aida, $5\frac{1}{2}$ stitches per cm ($13\frac{1}{2}$ stitches per in)
Cutting size: 30×12 cm ($11\frac{3}{4} \times 4\frac{3}{4}$ in)
Finished size: $5\frac{1}{2} \times 24$ cm ($2\frac{1}{4} \times 9\frac{1}{2}$ in)
Thread: DMC embroidery floss. Use 2 strands in the needle

Sew the four designs with space for 5 stitches in between.

JAR COVERS
Cutting size: 15×15 cm (6×6 in)
Lace: 45 cm ($17\frac{3}{4}$ in)

PLATE LINER
Material: beige Aida, $4\frac{1}{2}$ stitches per cm (11 stitches per in)
Cutting size: 16×16 cm ($6\frac{1}{4} \times 6\frac{1}{4}$ in)
Lace: 50 cm ($19\frac{3}{4}$ in)
Thread: DMC embroidery floss. Use 3 strands in the needle

NAPKIN HOLDER
Material: Aida, $5\frac{1}{2}$ stitches per cm ($13\frac{1}{2}$ stitches per in)
Cutting size: 12×18 cm ($4\frac{3}{4} \times 7$ in)
Finished size: 5 cm (2 in) deep
Thread: DMC embroidery floss. Use 2 strands in the needle

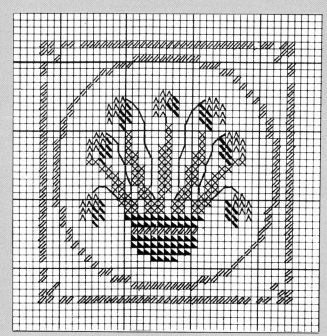

◣ 632 brown	⌒ 906 (backstitch)	⊟ 553 lilac
⌒ 632 (backstitch)	⊡ 741 orange	⊞ 554 light lilac
Ⅱ 782 golden brown	⊙ 973 dark yellow	⦀ 333 blue
⊘ 832 golden	L 307 light yellow	⊠ 340 light blue
- - - 832 (backstitch)	◣ 892 red	▼ 921 rust
⊠ 906 green	∧ 957 pink	

RED TULIPS

PICTURE

Material: Aida, $5\frac{1}{2}$ stitches per cm
($13\frac{1}{2}$ stitches per in)
Cutting size: 18×20 cm ($7 \times 7\frac{3}{4}$ in)
Finished size: (inside frame)
16×13 cm ($6\frac{1}{4} \times 5$ in)
Thread: DMC embroidery floss. Use
2 strands in the needle

DECORATIVE BORDER
FOR LAMPSHADE

Material: Aida, $5\frac{1}{2}$ stitches per cm
($13\frac{1}{2}$ stitches per in)
Cutting size: 12 cm ($4\frac{3}{4}$ in) $\times$
circumference of lampshade
Finished size: 8 cm ($3\frac{1}{4}$ in) deep

NAPKIN/PLATE LINER

Material: Aida, $5\frac{1}{2}$ stitches per cm
($13\frac{1}{2}$ stitches per in)
Cutting size: 18×18 cm (7×7 in)
Finished size: 16.5 cm ($6\frac{1}{2}$ in)
Bias binding: 70 cm ($27\frac{1}{2}$ in)
Thread: DMC embroidery floss. Use
2 strands in the needle

SPECTACLE CASE

Material: Aida, $5\frac{1}{2}$ stitches per cm
($13\frac{1}{2}$ stitches per in)
Cutting size: $2 \times 11 \times 18$ cm
($4\frac{1}{2} \times 7$ in)
Finished size: 10×15 cm (4×6 in)
Bias binding: 65 cm ($25\frac{1}{2}$ in)

RUNNER

Material: Aida, $5\frac{1}{2}$ stitches per cm
($13\frac{1}{2}$ stitches per in)
Cutting size: 21×55 cm
($8\frac{1}{4} \times 21\frac{3}{4}$ in)
Finished size: 17×50 cm
($6\frac{3}{4} \times 19\frac{3}{4}$ in)

◣	580 dark green	⊡	349 medium red
◿	470 medium green	☒	892 light red
Ｌ	471 light green	⊟	3326 pink
⊙	725 yellow	—	3266 (pink backstitch)
■	347 dark red		

TREES AND FLOWERS

TEA COSY
Material: beige Aida, $4\frac{1}{2}$ stitches per cm (11 stitches per in)
Batting
Lining
Bias binding (pink)

Make a pattern for your cosy and draw the outline on the fabric. Before starting the work, decide how the design should be placed. The cosy in the photo is 24×20 cm ($9\frac{1}{2} \times 7\frac{3}{4}$ in).

Press the finished embroidery. Make a sandwich with the embroidery, batting and linen, and baste all three pieces together. Machine- or hand-sew about 0.5 cm ($\frac{1}{4}$ in) from the outline, leaving lower edge open. Trim excess seam allowance. Repeat for the back. Hold back and front of cosy together, and baste shaped outside edges together. Turn hem at lower edge to inside and sew in place. Sew the bias binding over the edges (see photo).

TRAY CLOTH
Material: beige Aida, $4\frac{1}{2}$ stitches per cm (11 stitches per in)
Cutting size: 28×38 cm (11×15 in).
Fringe 2 cm ($\frac{3}{4}$ in)
Thread: DMC embroidery floss. Use 3 strands in the needle

POT HOLDER
Material: beige Aida, $4\frac{1}{2}$ stitches per cm (11 stitches per in)
Cutting size: 18×18 cm (7×7 in) (2 pieces)
Finished size: 16.5×16.5 cm ($6\frac{1}{2} \times 6\frac{1}{2}$ in)
Bias binding: 70 cm ($27\frac{1}{2}$ in)
Batting: 16.5×16.5 cm ($6\frac{1}{2} \times 6\frac{1}{2}$ in)

◥ 611 brown	⊠ 341 light blue
~ 611 (backstitch)	⊓ 701 dark green
⊙ 350 red	⊠ 703 medium green
⋀ 957 pink	L 907 light green
⧄ 793 blue	− 907 (backstitch)

CURTAIN

Material: beige Aida, $4\frac{1}{2}$ stitches per cm (11 stitches per in)

Cutting size: 45 cm ($17\frac{3}{4}$ in) deep × the length you need

Thread: DMC embroidery floss. Use 3 strands in the needle

Begin to embroider 7 cm ($2\frac{3}{4}$ in) from the lower edge. Finish with a 2-cm ($\frac{3}{4}$-in) hem on the bottom and 1-cm ($\frac{1}{2}$-in) the other sides.

COFFEE-FILTER HOLDER

Material: beige Aida, $4\frac{1}{2}$ stitches per cm (11 stitches per in)

Cutting size: one piece 22 × 16 cm ($9 \times 6\frac{1}{4}$ in) and one smaller, 22 × 11 cm ($9 \times 4\frac{1}{2}$ in)

Bias binding: 80 cm ($31\frac{1}{2}$ in)

2 small plastic rings

Glue a piece of cardboard or iron interfacing onto the wrong side of the fabric. This will help keep the holder stiff.

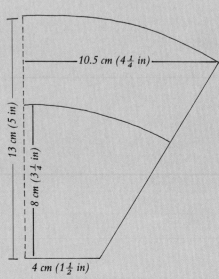

8

Kitchen Special

*F*or this section I have given only a few examples. The reason is that all plate liner designs can be used for pot holders and borders for shelves. The cover with violets shown on page 82 will be perfect for recipes. Protect the book with plastic so that the embroidery does not get damaged. If you mount it as shown, it will be easy to remove and clean it.

CURTAIN WITH BOWL OF FLOWERS

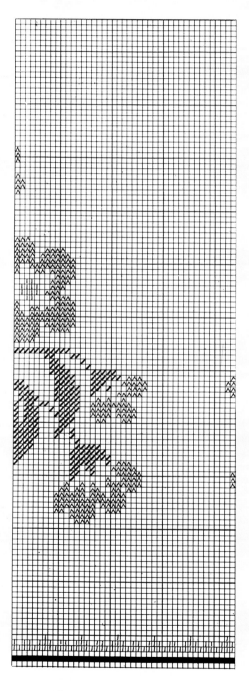

Material: beige Aida, $5\frac{1}{2}$ stitches per cm ($13\frac{1}{2}$ stitches per in)
Cutting size: 40 cm ($15\frac{3}{4}$ in) deep × the length you need
Curtain rings
Bias binding
Thread: DMC embroidery floss. Use 2 strands in the needle

☑ 987 green

⊞ 734 light yellowish green

■ 840 brown

⋀ 597 turquoise

Finish the embroidery with bias binding, 2 stitches from the border.

Before starting work, it is a good idea to plan out how the flowers should be placed on the curtain. One bunch of flowers will measure 31×20 cm ($12\frac{1}{4} \times 7\frac{3}{4}$ in). It may be necessary to position them with a wider distance between the flowers than shown, to suit your window.

FLORAL OVENGLOVE

Material: beige Aida, $5\frac{1}{2}$ stitches per cm ($13\frac{1}{2}$ stitches per in)
Cutting size: 35×40 cm ($13\frac{3}{4} \times 15\frac{3}{4}$ in)
Terry-cloth or foam insulation Interfacing
Coloured bias binding: 45 cm ($17\frac{3}{4}$ in)
Thread: DMC embroidery floss. Use 2 strands in the needle

☑ 580 green

⊞ 734 light yellowish green

■ 840 brown

∧ 3328 red

Inside of glove: cut 2 layers of interfacing and 2 layers of terry-cloth, using the diagram as a pattern. Zigzag-stitch them together, keeping the terry-cloth outermost. **Outside of glove:** trace your pattern on the linen, and begin to embroider the border 2 cm ($\frac{3}{4}$ in) from the bottom.

Press the finished embroidery. Stitch the front and back together, right sides facing. Cut surplus linen 0.5 cm ($\frac{1}{4}$ in) from the outline, and insert the terry-cloth lining. Baste the bias binding over the sandwich of materials and zigzag-stitch them all together.

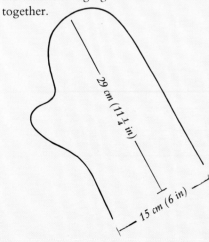

29 cm ($11\frac{1}{4}$ in)

15 cm (6 in)

OVENGLOVE WITH FORSYTHIA

Material: white Aida, $5\frac{1}{2}$ stitches per cm ($13\frac{1}{2}$ stitches per in)
Cutting size: (2 pieces) 35×20 cm ($13\frac{3}{4} \times 7\frac{3}{4}$ in)
Batting
Lining
Bias binding: 130 cm (51 in) 2.5 cm (1 in) wide
Thread: DMC embroidery floss. Use 2 strands in the needle

Press the finished embroidery. Layer embroidered pieces with right side on top, one piece of batting (foam insulation) and one piece of lining. Repeat for the back of the mitt. Baste all six pieces together; then, using the pattern as a guide, machine-stitch, leaving lower edge open. Trim excess fabric. Baste the bias tape all round, leaving excess for a loop, and machine-stitch.

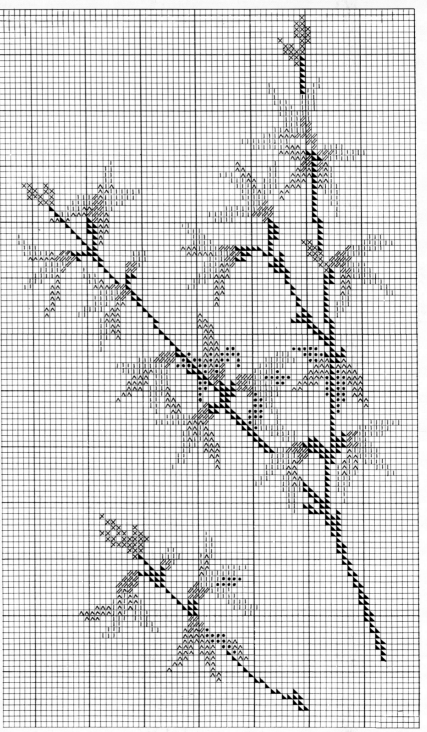

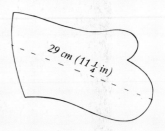

29 cm ($11\frac{1}{4}$ in)

- ◣ 611 brown
- ▨ 471 light green
- ⊠ 907 light bright green
- ● 725 dark yellow
- ⋀ 444 medium yellow
- ▯ 307 light yellow

9

Borders

A *border is one of the most useful designs imaginable. As you will see on the following pages, a border decorating a towel makes a pretty present for birthday or Christmas. Or you can make a belt in colours which match your dress, a frame for your favourite photo, a decoration for the shelves in your kitchen, or beautiful tray cloths and placemats. There are dozens of things you can embellish, according to your personal taste. As you can see from the photo, it is easy to make a corner for the embroidery by using a mirror, placed to reflect the border.*

BELT WITH PINK FLOWERS

Material: linen, 10 threads per cm
(25 threads per in)
Cutting size: 11 cm ($4\frac{1}{2}$ in) deep ×
size of waist
Finished size: 4 cm ($1\frac{1}{2}$ in) deep
Thread: DMC embroidery floss. Use
2 strands in the needle

Press the finished embroidery. Fold
the edges to the wrong side.
Allowing the two pieces of fabric to
overlap by about 0.5 cm ($\frac{1}{4}$ in), trim
away excess fabric. Sew back closed.
Trim top edges, fold raw edges to the
inside and sew in place. Insert the
strap.

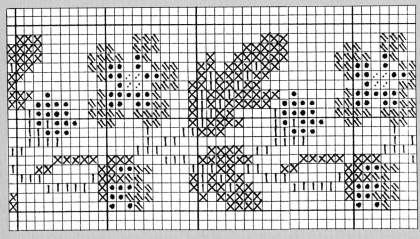

⊠ 470 dark green   ◩ 893 light red

▯▯ 471 light green   ⫶ 725 yellow

⊡ 601 dark red

BELT WITH STYLIZED FLOWERS

Material: Aida, $5\frac{1}{2}$ stitches per cm
($13\frac{1}{2}$ stitches per in)
Cutting size: 11 cm ($4\frac{1}{2}$ in)
deep × size of waist
Finished size: 4 cm ($1\frac{1}{2}$ in) deep
Thread: DMC embroidery floss. Use
3 strands in the needle

Press the finished embroidery. Fold
the edges to the wrong side.
Allowing the two pieces of fabric to
overlap by about 0.5 cm ($\frac{1}{4}$ in), trim
away excess fabric. Sew back closed.
Trim top edges, fold raw edges to the
inside and sew in place. Insert the
strap.

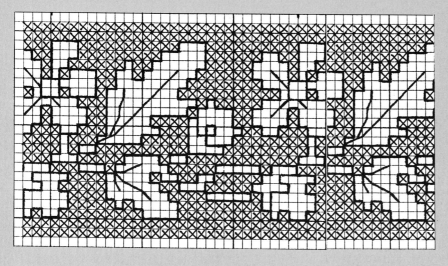

— 311 dark blue (backstitch)

⊠ 793 light blue

TULIP FRAME

Material: Aida, $5\frac{1}{2}$ stitches per cm
($13\frac{1}{2}$ stitches per in)
Foam rubber: 1 cm ($\frac{1}{2}$ in) thick
Cardboard: 2 mm ($\frac{1}{8}$ in) thick
Thread: DMC embroidery floss. Use
2 strands in the needle

- ● 907 green
- ◣ 900 dark orange
- ▨ 970 light orange
- ◿ 972 dark yellow
- ◻ 973 medium yellow
- ◺ 445 light yellow

Cut the cardboard 27.5 × 21.5 cm
($10\frac{3}{4} \times 8\frac{1}{2}$ in). The width of the frame
is 3 cm ($1\frac{1}{4}$ in).

Cut 3 cm ($1\frac{1}{4}$ in) wide strips of
foam rubber and glue them to the
cardboard frame before you fold the
embroidery round and sew the edges
together on the wrong side. Sew the
corner edges in place with small
stitches.

NB. All fabrics vary, so before cutting
out your cardboard, make sure that
your embroidery corresponds to the
measurements indicated.

NAPKIN HOLDER WITH THISTLES

Material: linen, 10 threads per cm
(25 threads per in)
Cutting size: 32 × 34 cm
($12\frac{1}{2}$ × $13\frac{1}{2}$ in)
Finished size, folded: 30 × 11 cm
($11\frac{3}{4}$ × $4\frac{1}{2}$ in)
Bias binding: 130 cm (51 in)
Thread: DMC embroidery floss. Use
2 strands in the needle

Begin to embroider the backstitch
line 1.5 cm ($\frac{5}{8}$ in) from the edges.
Embroider the motif on one short
side only, but stitch the border all
round. Press the finished embroidery
and trim fabric 10 threads away from
the border. Baste the bias binding on
and machine-stitch. Fold the finished
piece in three parts to form the
napkin holder, with the embroidery
on top. Sew the two underneath parts
together so that you have an
envelope to put the napkin in.

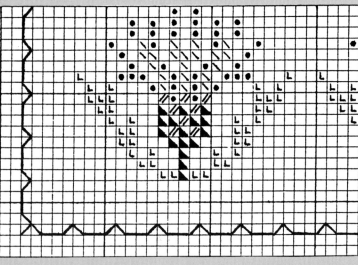

- ● 552 bluish lilac
- ◣ 917 reddish lilac
- ◥ 936 dark green
- ▨ 732 dull green
- – 732 (backstitch)
- L 907 bright light green

TULIP BORDER FOR SHELF

Material: Aida, $4\frac{1}{2}$ stitches per cm (11 stitches per in)
Cutting size: 14 cm ($5\frac{1}{2}$ in) × width of your towel
Thread: DMC embroidery floss. Use 3 strands in the needle

◼ 905 dark green

▨ 703 light green

● 892 dark pink

ʟ 957 light pink

∧ 209 lilac

Iron the finished embroidery and fold over the long sides to make a small hem.

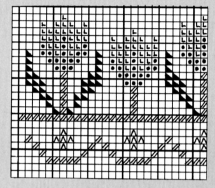

PINCUSHION WITH ROSES

Material: (2 pieces) 11 × 10 cm
($4\frac{1}{2}$ × 4 in)
Lace: 50 cm ($19\frac{3}{4}$ in)

Turn the edges to the wrong side and baste on the ruffled lace. Baste together the front and back, right sides facing, and machine-stitch together leaving a hole for stuffing. Turn to right side and fill with cotton wool or foam rubber. Stitch the opening.

ROSE BORDER FOR TOWELS

Material: Aida, $5\frac{1}{2}$ stitches per cm ($13\frac{1}{2}$ stitches per in)
Lace: 80 cm ($31\frac{1}{2}$ in)
Cutting size: 8 cm ($3\frac{1}{4}$ in) deep × width of your towel

Finished size: 5 cm (2 in) deep
Thread: DMC embroidery floss. Use 2 strands in the needle

Turn the edges to the wrong side, 4 stitches from the embroidery. Baste on the ruffled lace and machine-stitch in place.

■ 581 green

− 581 (backstitch)

▨ 907 bright green

● 892 dark pink

⋀ 3706 medium pink

⫙ 776 light pink

⋅ 726 yellow

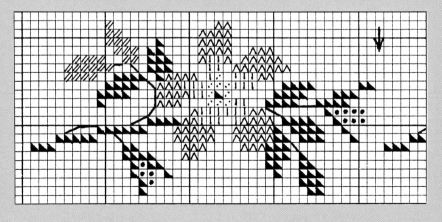

Material: beige Aida, $5\frac{1}{2}$ stitches per cm ($13\frac{1}{2}$ stitches per in)
Cutting size: 8 cm ($3\frac{1}{4}$ in) deep
Finished size: 5 cm (2 in) deep
Thread: DMC embroidery floss. Use 2 strands in the needle

- ⊡ 731 dull green
- ⊠ 906 green
- ⌶ 907 light green
- ◣ 801 brown
- – 801 (backstitch)
- ⟋ 720 dark orange
- ⊙ 970 medium orange
- ⬚ 741 light orange

Iron the finished embroidery. Fold over the long sides to make a small hem. Machine-stitch the border to your towel.

BUTTERFLY BORDER FOR TOWELS

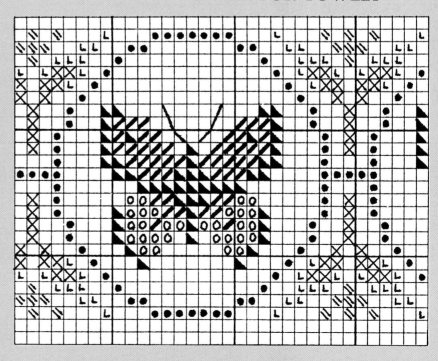

PERIWINKLE BORDER FOR TOWELS

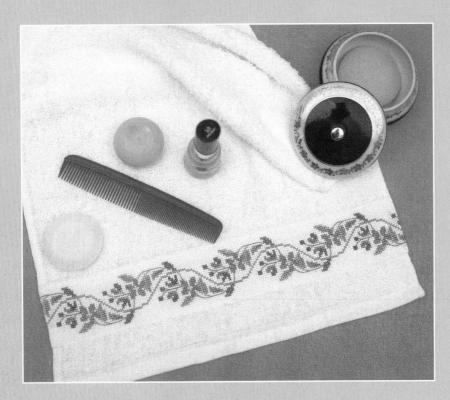

Material: Aida, $5\frac{1}{2}$ stitches per cm ($13\frac{1}{2}$ stitches per in)
Cutting size: 8 cm ($3\frac{1}{4}$ in) × width of your towel
Thread: DMC embroidery floss. Use 2 strands in the needle

- ● 680 brown
- ⋮ 444 yellow
- ◣ 905 dark green
- ▨ 906 medium green
- – 906 (backstitch)
- L 907 light green
- I 798 dark blue
- ∧ 799 light blue

Iron the finished embroidery and fold over the long sides to make a small hem. Machine-stitch the border to your towel.

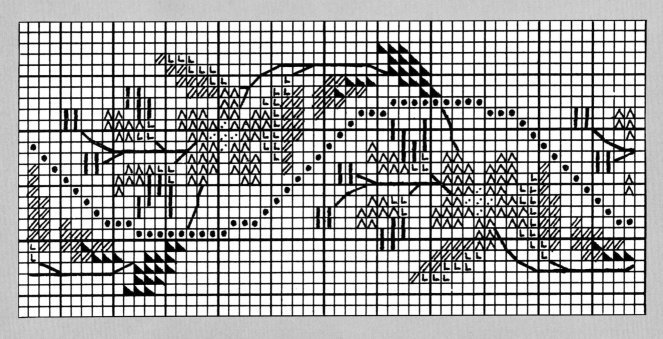

10

Small Useful Ideas

*I*n this section you will find small designs which you can embroider on dresses, collars, pockets, babies' bibs, scarfs, and so on. They are easily made with the help of canvas or similar stiff material. See instructions on page 8.

G IS FOR GUEST

Material: a piece of waste canvas, 8 × 10 cm (3¼ × 4 in), 4 stitches per cm (10¼ stitches per in)
Finished size: 6 × 5 cm (2½ × 2 in)
Thread: DMC embroidery floss. Use all 6 strands in the needle

◥ 799 blue

⊙ 603 dark pink

L 604 light pink

⋅ 744 yellow

◪ 733 dull green

∧ 471 light green

You can work the embroidery on non-evenweave fabric by using waste canvas. Follow the instructions on page 8.

TOWEL MOTIF WITH FLOWER AND RIBBON

Material: a piece of waste canvas, 14×14 cm ($5\frac{1}{2} \times 5\frac{1}{2}$ in), 4 stitches per cm ($10\frac{1}{2}$ stitches per in)
Finished size: $9\frac{1}{2} \times 11$ cm ($3\frac{3}{4} \times 4\frac{1}{2}$ in)
Thread: DMC embroidery floss. Use all 6 strands in the needle

- 988 dark green
- 3347 light green
- 603 dark pink
- 604 medium pink
- 776 light pink
- 725 yellow
- 553 dark lilac
- 554 light lilac

You can work the embroidery on non-evenweave fabric by using waste canvas. Follow the instructions on page 8.

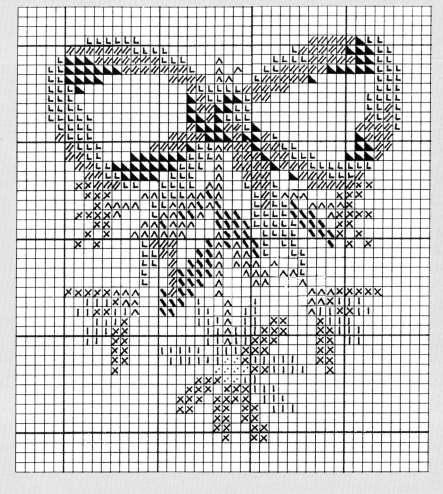

WREATH FOR CUSHION

Material: a piece of waste canvas 15 × 11 cm (6 × 4½ in) with 4½ stitches per cm (11 stitches per in)
Finished size: 10.5 × 8 cm (4¼ × 3¼ in)
Thread: DMC embroidery floss. Use 3 strands in the needle

◤	470 dark green
∧	907 light green
⊙	340 dark blue
L	341 light blue
⊡	726 yellow

You can work the embroidery on non-evenweave fabric by using waste canvas. Follow the instructions on page 8.

BOUQUET MOTIF

Material: a piece of waste canvas,
8×8 cm $(3\frac{1}{4} \times 3\frac{1}{4}$ in), 5 stitches per
cm (13 stitches per in)
Finished size: 5.5×5.5 cm
$(2\frac{1}{4} \times 2\frac{1}{4}$ in)
Thread: DMC embroidery floss. Use
2 strands in the needle

You can work the embroidery on
non-evenweave fabric by using waste
canvas. Follow the instructions on
page 8.

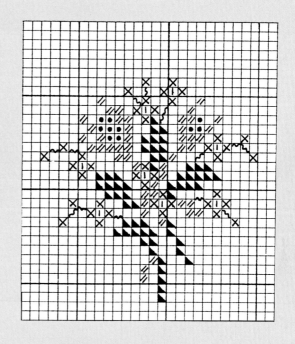

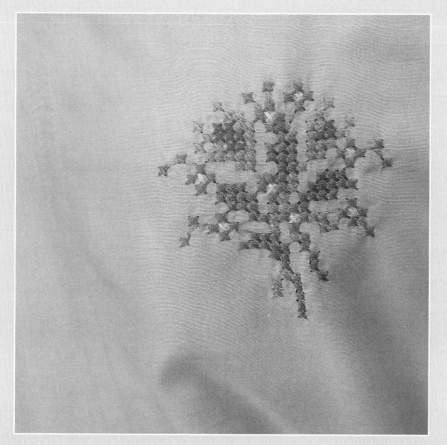

- ◣ 3346 dark green
- ▨ 3347 light green
- ~ 3347 (backstitch)
- ● 601 red
- ⊠ 553 lilac
- Ⅱ 726 yellow

BUTTONS, BROOCH AND EARRINGS

Material: linen, 10 threads per cm
(25 threads per in)
Plastic rings or buttons
Thread: DMC embroidery floss. Use
2 strands in the needle

PANSY

- ◣ 3021 dark brown
- ◻ 915 dark red
- ⊠ 309 medium red
- ⊡ 892 light red
- ⊟ 906 green
- ⊙ 972 orange
- ⊡ 3078 yellow

TULIPS

- ⊙ 601 dark pink
- ⊡ 603 light pink
- ◣ 987 dark green
- ⊘ 989 light green

BLUEBELLS

- ◣ 987 dark green
- ⊘ 989 light green
- – 989 (backstitch)
- ⊙ 333 dark blue
- ⊡ 340 light blue

For these tiny embroideries, sew in
petit-point (only over one thread!).
To make up, mark the ring (or
button) outline on the linen and
make basting stitches 0.5 cm ($\frac{1}{4}$ in)
around. Put the ring inside and pull
the yarn tight. Cut away excess fabric
and sew several stitches in different
directions to get a smooth surface.

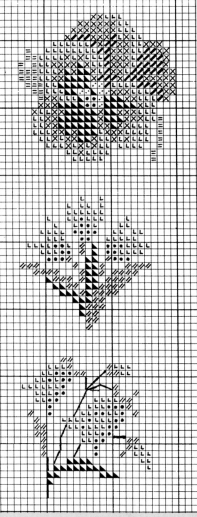

SMARTEN UP WITH FLOWERS

Material: a piece of waste canvas, $4\frac{1}{2}$ stitches per cm (11 stitches per in)
Finished size: Bluebell: 3.5×7.5 cm ($1\frac{1}{2} \times 3$ in); **Pansy:** 4.5×7.5 cm ($1\frac{3}{4} \times 3$ in); **Winter aconite:** 6×9.5 cm ($2\frac{1}{2} \times 3\frac{3}{4}$ in)
Thread: DMC embroidery floss. Use 3 strands in the needle

You can work the embroidery on non-evenweave fabric by using waste canvas. Follow the instructions on page 8.

BLUEBELL

◣ 987 dark green

⊞ 906 light green

— 906 (backstitch)

⦿ 333 dark blue

L 340 light blue

⧄ 932 greyish blue

310 black. backstitch: sew with only one thread over the cross stitches as marked on the design.

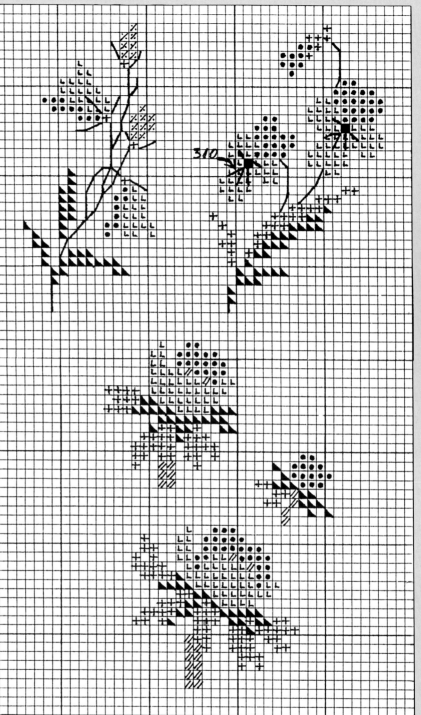

PANSY

◣ 987 dark green

⊞ 906 light green

— 906 (backstitch)

⦿ 553 lilac

■ 741 orange

L 973 yellow

WINTER ACONITE

◣ 987 dark green

⊞ 906 light green

⧄ 734 yellowish green

⦿ 725 dark yellow

L 973 light yellow

MOTIF FOR BABY CLOTHES

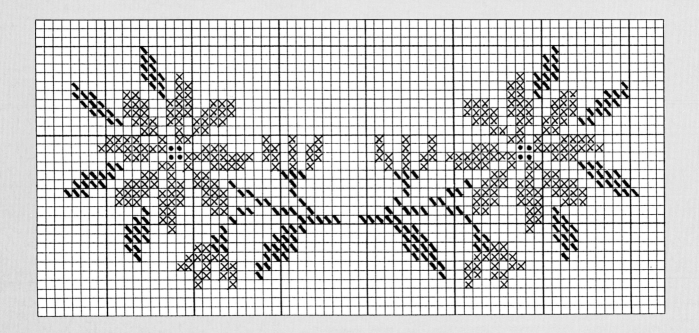

Material: a piece of waste canvas, 10 × 8 cm (4 × 3¼ in) for each bouquet, 5 stitches per cm (13 stitches per in)

Finished size: 7.5 × 5.5 cm (3 × 2¼ in)

Thread: DMC embroidery floss. Use 3 strands in the needle

⊠ white

⊙ 727 yellow

◩ 471 green

You can work the embroidery on non-evenweave fabric by using waste canvas. Follow the instructions on page 8.

BABY'S BIB

Material: Aida, $4\frac{1}{2}$ stitches per cm
(11 stitches per in)
Cutting size: 30×24 cm
($11\frac{3}{4} \times 9\frac{1}{2}$ in)
Eyelet edging: 120 cm (47 in)
Thread: DMC embroidery floss. Use
3 strands in the needle

Making-up instructions are given on
page 9.

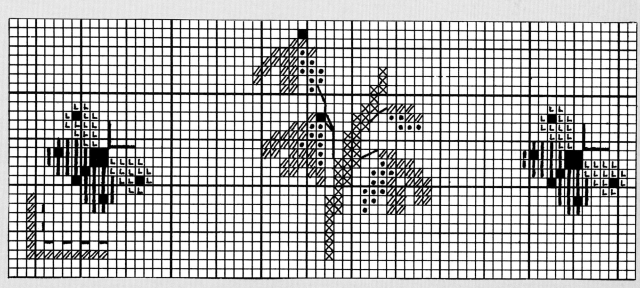

☒ 906 green	▨ 799 light blue *or* 604 light pink	⌊ 444 yellow
⦿ 798 dark blue *or* 603 dark pink	⨅ 742 orange	■ 840 brown
		— 840 (backstitch)

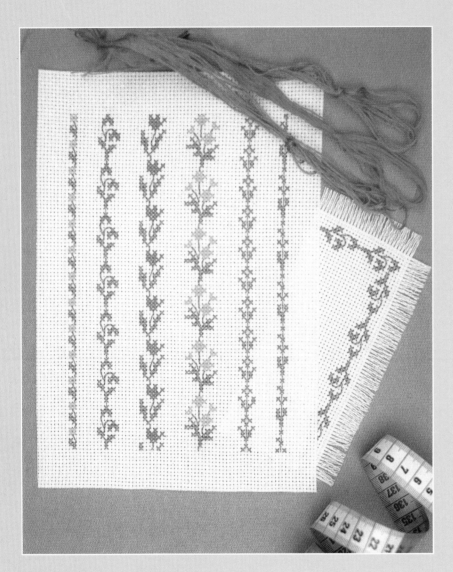

BORDERS

Material: white Aida, $4\frac{1}{2}$ stitches per cm (11 stitches per in)
Thread: DMC embroidery floss. Use 3 strands in the needle

- ● 340 blue
- ◣ 209 lilac
- ⊓ 603 red
- ▨ 972 dark yellow
- ⧄ 727 light yellow
- ⊠ 906 green
- ···· 906 (backstitch)

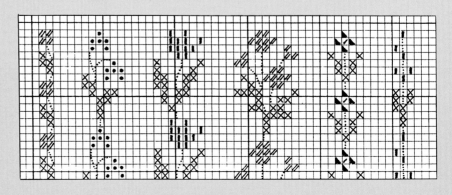

MATCHBOX COVER WITH WILD ROSE

Material: linen, 10 threads per cm (25 threads per in)
Cutting size: 18×12 cm ($7 \times 4\frac{3}{4}$ in)
Thread: DMC embroidery floss. Use 2 strands in the needle

◥ 501 dark bluish green

▨ 502 light bluish green

⋀ 988 dark green

⌊ 989 light green

■ 801 brown

⊙ 782 golden

Ⅲ 601 dark pink

⊠ 603 medium pink

⊟ 604 light pink

⊡ 818 very light pink

BOX COVER WITH BOWL OF FLOWERS

Material: linen, 8 threads per cm (20 threads per in)
Cutting size: 20 × 15 cm (7¾ × 6 in)
Finished size: 18.5 × 12.5 cm (7¼ × 5 in)
Bias binding: 65 cm (25½ in)
Thread: DMC embroidery floss. Use 3 strands in the needle

◤ 434 brown

◿ 904 dark green

☒ 906 light green

− 906 (backstitch)

⊙ 304 dark red

‖ 891 medium red

L 956 rose

⋄ 444 yellow

Cut a piece of cardboard as the cover. Iron the finished embroidery and wrap it around the cardboard. Fasten with glue. Glue on the bias binding.

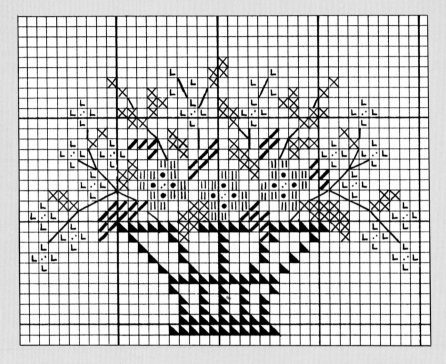

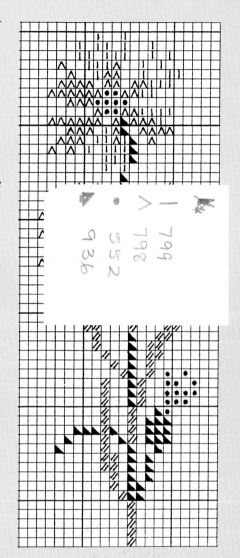

BOOKMARK WITH CHRYSANTHEMUM

Material: linen, 10 threads per cm (25 threads per in)
Cutting size: 10 × 16 cm (4 × 6¼ in)
Finished size: 4 × 16 cm (1½ × 6¼ in)
Thread: DMC embroidery floss. Use 2 strands in the needle

- ◣ 904 dark green
- ⊘ 470 light green
- ⊙ 780 brown
- ⋀ 742 dark yellow
- ⫿ 973 light yellow

Iron the finished embroidery. Fold the long edges to the wrong side, overlap slightly and stitch neatly in place. Make a fringe of about 2 cm (¾ in) at the top and bottom by removing threads.

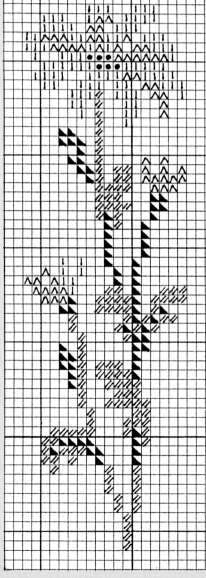

BOOKMARK WITH CORNFLOWER

Material: linen, 10 threads per cm (25 threads per in)
Cutting size: 10 × 16 cm (4 × 6¼ in)
Finished size: 4 × 16 cm (1½ × 6¼ in)
Thread: DMC embroidery floss. Use 2 strands in the needle

- ◣ 936 dark green
- ⊘ 470 light green
- ⊙ 552 lilac
- ⋀ 798 dark blue
- ⫿ 799 light blue

Iron the finished embroidery. Fold the long edges to the wrong side, overlap slightly and stitch neatly in place. Make a fringe of about 2 cm (¾ in) at the top and bottom by removing threads.

TISSUE HOLDER WITH MARIGOLD

Material: linen, 10 threads per cm
(25 threads per in)
Cutting size: 30 × 16 cm
$(11\frac{3}{4} \times 6\frac{1}{4}$ in)
Finished size: 14 × 14.5 cm
$(5\frac{1}{2} \times 5\frac{3}{4}$ in)
Bias binding: 60 cm (24 in)
Thread: DMC embroidery floss. Use
2 strands in the needle

◥ 986 dark green

◿ 905 medium green

⌃ 907 light green

■ 919 dark rust

⊡ 720 light rust

▯ 972 yellow

⊡ 444 light yellow

Find the centre and begin to
embroider the design 1 cm $(\frac{1}{2}$ in)
from there and 2.5 cm (1 in) from the
top. Press the finished embroidery
and turn the edges to the inside
making two envelopes to put the
tissues in. Baste on the bias binding
and machine-stitch.

7 cm $(2\frac{3}{4}$ in)

14.5 cm $(5\frac{3}{4}$ in)

SPECTACLE CASE

Material: beige Aida, $5\frac{1}{2}$ stitches per cm ($13\frac{1}{2}$ stitches per in)
Cutting size: 70×12 cm ($27\frac{1}{2} \times 4\frac{3}{4}$ in)
Finished size: 40×12 cm ($15\frac{3}{4} \times 4\frac{3}{4}$ in)
Bias binding: 110 cm (43 in)
Thread: DMC embroidery floss. Use 2 strands in the needle

◤ 904 dark green

◨ 906 medium green

⋀ 907 light green

● 915 reddish lilac

◪ 891 red

L 893 pink

− 893 (backstitch)

○ 407 beige

∼ 407 (backstitch)

Fold the fabric in half lengthwise to find the middle. Measure 1.5 cm ($\frac{5}{8}$ in) from the top of the fabric and begin to embroider at the arrow on the graph. Iron the finished embroidery and make small pockets at both ends, folding about 14 cm ($5\frac{1}{2}$ in). Machine-stitch on the bias binding.

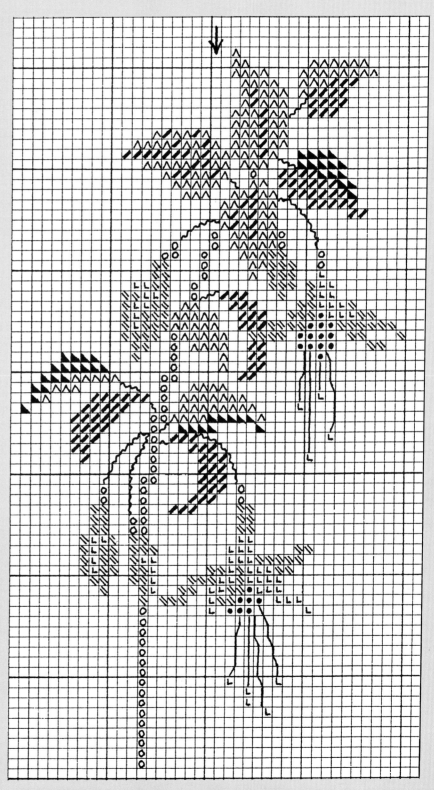

NAPKIN HOLDER WITH DAFFODIL

Material: linen, 10 threads per cm (25 threads per in)
Cutting size: 12 × 12 cm (4¾ × 4¾ in)
Finished size: 5 cm (2 in) deep
Lace: 40 cm (15¾ in)
Thread: DMC embroidery floss. Use 2 strands in the needle

◣ 987 dark green

▨ 989 light green

▥ 734 light yellowish green

◩ 900 dark orange

☒ 970 light orange

◉ 444 yellow

Ⓛ 727 light yellow

Iron the embroidery, put the ends together—right sides facing one another—and sew them together. Fold the linen on the wrong side, and sew the edges together. Reverse, and sew on the lace.

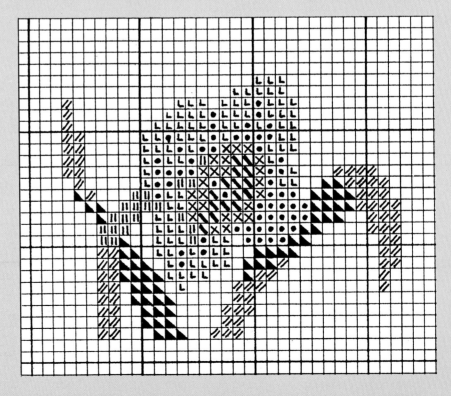

11

Christmas Designs

*Y*ou can mount the wreath with poinsettia on a piece of cardboard and hang it on the door. Your guests will definitely admire it! The motif on the napkin ring can be sewn on a piece of fine linen, with a 6 mm ($\frac{1}{4}$ in) fringe on all four sides. You can also use it for Christmas cards or birthday greetings. Just glue the motif to cardboard, and you will have a personal greeting for relatives and friends in no time.

CHRISTMAS DECORATION WITH POINSETTIA

Material: linen, 10 threads per cm
(25 threads per in)
Cutting size: 25 × 30 cm
($9\frac{3}{4}$ × $11\frac{3}{4}$ in)
Finished size: about 20.5 × 25 cm
(8 × $9\frac{3}{4}$ in)
Cord: 90 cm ($35\frac{1}{2}$ in)
Cardboard: about 20.5 × 25 cm
(8 × $9\frac{3}{4}$ in)
Thread: DMC embroidery floss. Use
2 strands in the needle

Press the finished embroidery. Cut
the cardboard 1 cm ($\frac{3}{8}$ in) wider than
the embroidery and fold the fabric
around. Glue it to the wrong side and
sew on the cord (see photo).

- ● 904 dark green
- ∥ 988 medium green
- ⊠ 704 light green
- ■ 680 light brown
- ⊡ 734 light yellowish green
- ⊡ 725 yellow
- ◣ 498 dark red
- ◪ 321 medium red
- △ 891 light red
- ⊥ 892 very light red

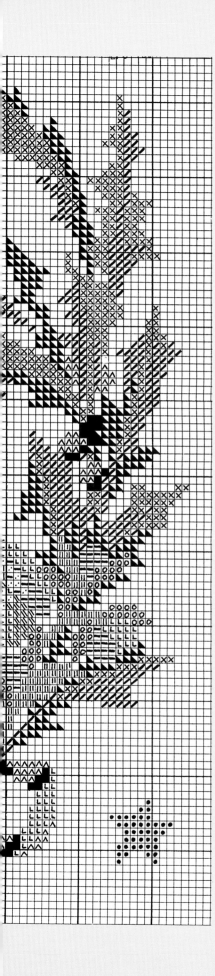

Tray cloth with Christmas rose and holly

◣	986 dark green
◿	905 medium green
⊠	906 light green
⊡	581 yellowish green
▯	3012 dull green
●	972 dark yellow
⊡	744 light yellow
⊟	3350 dark dull red
◩	3687 medium dull red
⌊	962 light dull red
■	321 red
⌃	350 medium red

Material: linen, 8 threads per cm (20 threads per in)
Cutting size (and finished size): 45 × 35 cm (17¾ × 13¾ in)
Bias binding: 170 cm (63 in), 2.5 cm (1 in) wide
Thread: DMC embroidery floss. Use 3 strands in the needle

Begin to embroider the stars in the corners, 3 cm (1¼ in) from the edges. Press the finished embroidery and baste the bias binding all round. Machine-stitch in place.

Napkin holder with poinsettia

Material: linen, 10 threads per cm
(25 threads per in)
Cutting size: 10 × 12 cm (4 × 4¾ in)
Finished size: 4 cm (1½ in) deep
Cord: 30 cm (11¾ in)
Thread: DMC embroidery floss. Use
2 strands in the needle

◪	987 dark green
▥	989 medium green
⊙	471 light green
■	221 dark reddish brown
☒	309 dark red
L	982 medium red
⋅	725 yellow

Iron the embroidery, put the ends
together—right sides facing one
another—and sew them together.
Fold the linen on the wrong side, and
sew the edges together. Reverse, and
sew on the cord.

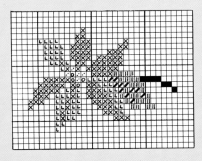

Holiday cloth

To hem, fold over 5 and then 12
threads to the wrong side of the
work and sew with small stitches.

Material: linen, 10 threads per cm
(25 threads per in)
Cutting size: 46 × 46 cm (18 × 18 in)
Finished size: 40 × 40 cm
(15¾ × 15¾ in)
Thread: DMC embroidery floss. Use
2 strands in the needle

◣	501 dark green
◪	988 medium green
◠	703 light green
⦿	3012 dull green
−	3012 (backstitch)
⋅	725 yellow
⊟	304 dark red
▥	891 medium red
L	893 light red

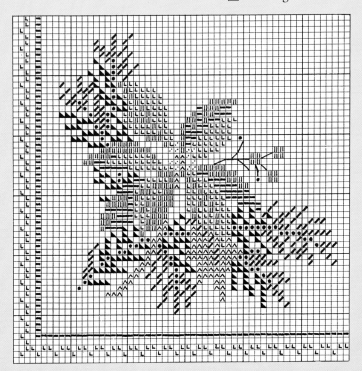